Copyright © Hood Hood Books
Hood Hood Books
46 Clabon Mews
London SW1X OEH
Tel: 44.171.5847878
Fax: 44.171.2250386

British Library Cataloguing–in–Publication Data
A catalogue record for this book is available from the British Library

ISBN 1 900251 13 2

Origination: Fine Line Graphics
Printed by IPH, Egypt

SULEIMAN

THE MAGNIFICENT
&
THE STORY OF ISTANBUL

Julia Marshall

Illustrated by Joan Ullathorne

HOOD HOOD BOOKS

Suleiman *the* Magnificent

A GREAT MAN

SULEIMAN, SULTAN OF THE MOST POWERFUL EMPIRE IN THE WORLD, arranged himself more comfortably on the golden cushions. Ambassadors from the West were to be presented to him that morning. They had come all the way from foreign lands, from Venice, from France and Hungary, to see the court of Suleiman the Magnificent as he was known in the West. He would not disappoint them, he would show them what they expected to see. That morning, on being woken by his attendants and while preparing himself for the first prayers of the day, he had felt his body ache with tiredness. He knew that his face was paler than ever and he had instructed one of his personal attendants to coat his skin with a layer of rouge. It would never do for foreign powers to learn that he was ill. He must appear fit and strong so that he could still inspire fear in their hearts. Any rumour that he was ill and his enemies would be waiting like vultures for his death, ready to pick over the bones of all of his triumphs as ruler of the great city of Istanbul, and the even greater Ottoman Empire.

Suleiman reached for a goblet encrusted with jewels and sipped the sweetened water it contained. He fingered the pearl buttons of his gown of green mohair and allowed his eyes to move around the richly decorated room that shone with the splendour of gold, silver and purple. There would be much to delight the eyes of these foreign ambassadors. They would notice the gold rose set with one large, perfect ruby that decorated his turban and the beautiful pearl, shaped like a pear that dangled from his right ear. They would see the stern expression with which he faced the world, the expression of a feared and admired leader. But they would never guess what lay hidden in his heart. His secrets were locked up deep inside him, and all those who had once held keys, all those he had once loved, were now dead and gone.

The great man sighed deeply but silently, so that no one would notice. The high price of greatness is never to be alone, but often to feel lonely. He was always surrounded by the bustle of attendants at court, or troops of soldiers on campaigns. It was only with his beloved wife, Roxelana, that he had been able to let the mask of greatness slip from his face. He would always remember the smile of his lovely laughing one, Khurrem, as he used to call her. But death had taken the smile from her face. She had gone to another world where one day he would be reunited with her. But for the moment he was alone in this world. Death had taken not only his wife, but his childhood friend, Ibrahim, and several of his sons. "Greatness is like a sleek, black panther," Suleiman thought to himself, taking another sip of the sweetened water to cool his throat. "It is fascinating, but it is greedy and needs cruel acts to keep itself alive. Greatness always demands to come first, before anything else in life. I thank God that I am wise enough in my old age to know that greatness has a place only in this world. When I leave this life, I will take none of these riches that surround me now; the magnificence that these foreign ambassadors come to look at with their gleaming eyes will not be important. It is time, now that I am getting old, to think back on my life, my mistakes, my triumphs and achievements, my joys and sorrows."

Suleiman closed his eyes for a moment and the picture that came to him was of the city of Istanbul, a queen among cities. He loved it with a passion. It was the jewel in the crown of his empire. "I will try," he thought, "to see my city with new eyes. I will imagine what it must be like for these foreign ambassadors, visiting it for the first time. They have been waiting three days to be presented to me as is the custom and during that time they will have seen some of the city. How rich in colour it must seem to them after the cold skies of their own western countries! I have not seen all the cities in the world, yet I cannot imagine one more beautiful than Istanbul. It stands so proudly, surrounded by seven hills, rising between the Sea of Marmara and the blue waters of the Golden Horn. Dark green cypresses cover the hills, reaching right to the massive walls that protect our city. Set against the sky is the great dome of the Aya Sofya, the most wonderful of all mosques. Formerly a great cathedral, it stands out as a reminder of the day my great-grandfather, Mehmet the Conqueror, took

Constantinople from its Christian rulers and made it Istanbul, capital of the Ottoman Empire. That was a great and terrible day in our history, a day of death and triumph. But from that day the Ottomans have ruled Istanbul, and the hundreds of tall minarets that reach from the mosques to the heavens give proof of our gratitude to God in allowing us to be the guardians of this city."

Suleiman forgot for a moment where he was and drifted off into a dream, imagining himself to be a young, healthy man, a man like any other, walking through the busy streets of the bustling city. In the dusty, narrow streets smelling of hyacinths, tulips and roses from the surrounding gardens, he heard the shouts of the streetsellers and the tradesmen going about their work. He saw the brightly coloured houses that opened onto the streets: yellow and red houses for Turks, purple for Jews, grey for Greeks and Armenians. Anyone was welcome to live in the great city of Istanbul, provided that they went about their lives peacefully and paid their taxes - in fact there were seventy different nationalities living there. Yes, Suleiman thought, almost allowing a smile to settle on his face, Istanbul was a jewel of a city and he was indeed fortunate that God had allowed him to be one of its rulers. Some years before he had ordered the great architect, Sinan, to build a mosque that would stand long after his death as proof of his devotion to God and to his people. The Suleimaniye, as it was called, stood on the highest hill in Istanbul, its ten galleries and four beautiful minarets, a reminder to everyone that Suleiman was the tenth ruler of the Ottoman Dynasty and the fourth to rule over the city of Istanbul.

Suleiman was forced to turn his mind away from thoughts of his city. The foreign ambassadors were waiting to see him. Carefully, he altered his expression so that it bore no trace of what he had been thinking and it became once more the dignified countenance of a formidable leader. Three ambassadors dressed in the fashion of the European courts were conducted by a scarlet-robed chamberlain into the presence of the great Sultan. All of them bowed the deepest of bows before Suleiman rose and held out his hand, as was his custom, for each of the men to kiss in turn. The first, he noticed, had an ugly wart just near his mouth. There was nothing noticeable about the second, a dull looking man, and the Sultan's eyes brushed dismissively over him. But the third was a man with an intelligent face and bright eyes that seemed to stare straight through everything he looked at. "He interests me, this man," the Sultan thought. "What does he see when he looks at me?"

Suleiman presented the three ambassadors with valuable gifts, rich robes, exquisitely-worked gold and costly jewels. He watched as the faces of the first two men glowed with greed. "This is what they came for," he thought. "It is stories of wondrous riches, luxurious living and cruel, bloody battles that they will take back to their countries to delight the ears of their listeners. This is what people in foreign lands want to hear about the Ottomans. They believe us to be warlike and decadent. Well, they can believe what they like, but I have a feeling that this third man, this de Busbeq as he is called, might want to learn something of the truth of Suleiman and the people he rules." By the time the three ambassadors had once again performed their deep bows and withdrawn from the presence of the great Sultan, Suleiman had decided that he would find time to talk to this man with the bright eyes.

AN INVITATION TO THE IMPERIAL AMBASSADOR

D E BUSBEQ, THE AMBASSADOR TO FERDINAND I OF HUNGARY, COULD hardly contain his excitement as he was handed the parchment by a royal page. The letter was wrapped in cloth of gold and there was no doubt that it came from the Sultan himself. De Busbeq had been invited for a few days hunting at the Sultan's private retreat across the Bosphorus. This was indeed an unusual honour. De Busbeq felt a small stab of fear mingling with the excitement that swept through him. In his country there was no man more feared than Suleiman the Magnificent. It was not so many years ago that their countries had been at war with each other. Now there was official peace, but there were many who remembered the Ottoman army, the best army in the world, united in their allegiance to the

Sultan and prepared to die for him. However, suppressing his own feelings, de Busbeq bowed low before the royal messenger and gave his grateful acceptance.

The next day they departed. Reclining on mattresses of gold and silver, they sailed in one of the luxurious royal barques across the clear blue waters of the Bosphorus to the gardens on the other side. It was a warm day, the quiet air was filled with the scent of orange blossom. Although de Busbeq could never be alone with the Sultan, Suleiman had, that day, surrounded himself with his favourite personal attendants whom he could rely upon to keep silent on any matter he might choose to discuss.

"So," Suleiman spoke, breaking the stillness of the perfumed air, "tell me what impressions you have formed of my city."

De Busbeq hesitated for a moment. He did not want to say the wrong thing to such a powerful man. But he also knew that such a great man would know if he were not telling the truth and he decided to answer quite honestly.

"I am overwhelmed, my lord," he said, "in truth I have never seen so many people. Indeed, I have learnt that there are more than seven hundred thousand people living in Istanbul – that is, more than in any other great city of the world."

Suleiman nodded. "That is correct."

"And another thing, my lord," de Busbeq continued, "it is a strange thing for me to see people of so many different religions living in peace together. As you know, Europe is torn by religious wars with Christians fighting Christians. Henry VIII of England has broken away from the Church of Rome and it seems as if no one can agree with anyone else."

Suleiman seemed to give a ghost of a smile, but by the time de

Busbeq examined his face more clearly, it had vanished and it was only the grave mask that met his eyes.

"That is the secret," the great ruler spoke solemnly, "that is the great secret of the success of the Ottoman Empire, my empire. We are not divided. Supreme authority rests with me alone and I have complete control." He paused for a moment and then said, "Did you know that the people who help me run this great empire are all slaves. The men who fight in my army to extend my kingdom and spread the Muslim faith, the men who run the government and apply the laws that I have decreed, the women who bear my children – they are all slaves."

De Busbeq was silent, he did not know how to answer. Suleiman continued. "I know that in the West, you believe slavery to be a shameful and humiliating state. But it is not so with us. We believe that talent must have a chance to show itself before it withers. It should sparkle in the sun so that all can see its brilliance. So every few years I send out the officers of my army, the commanders of the janissaries. They stop in all the large towns of my empire. The *qadis* or judges of the town gather together all the boys aged between eight and eighteen and the officers then select the strongest and most intelligent of them to take to Istanbul for training." Suleiman must have noticed the strange look that passed over the face of de Busbeq.

"Oh, do not misunderstand," he said gravely. "These boys are not taken by force. If any boy is an only son, married or needed by his family because of his skills, he is not taken. Moreover, it is the wish of almost every boy to be chosen. That way he can make something of his life, he can come to court, receive an education and, if he has true intelligence, he can even rise to the most powerful position in the kingdom after mine, that of Grand Vizier. That is what happened with my oldest and closest friend, Ibrahim. We were childhood companions, he a slave, and I the heir to the throne, and yet he became almost as powerful as I did."

De Busbeq noticed a look of deep sadness pass quickly over the face of the Sultan. He knew that Suleiman had ordered the death of Ibrahim; people whispered about it, but de Busbeq did not think he could possibly ask the great Sultan any questions about the Grand Vizier, Ibrahim. Instead, he continued to ask about the collection of these boys for the service of the empire. The *devshirme* system it was called which means 'the gathering'. Suleiman was happy to explain.

"Up to three thousand boys are collected at any one time. They are then divided into groups of a hundred, dressed in special robes and sent to Istanbul. The best are chosen for service in my palace and sent to a special school where they learn Arabic, Persian and Osmanli, the languages that every Ottoman should be familiar with. They read the Qur'an and are taught law. Some of these boys, only the very best, become my personal attendants. Others become governors of provinces or part of my mounted bodyguard, the *sipahis* as they are called. Those who are not up to the standard for palace service become janissaries, members of my loyal fighting troops."

De Busbeq nodded and watched the Sultan with his bright eyes.

"You see," Suleiman said, his voice lowering slightly, "these boys leave everything behind when they come into my service; their homes, families, even their religion. They become Muslims and are dedicated to me and the Muslim faith. Their training is harsh and difficult, but they are well looked after, given scarlet garments twice a year, and robes of white for summer. When they leave the palace to serve me and the empire, I give them an embroidered coat, a horse and my blessing. From then on, it is their talent that will make their fortune."

The magnificent boat was now reaching the other side and Suleiman's personal attendants were preparing to help their Sultan ashore. As he rose, Suleiman turned towards de Busbeq. "We Ottomans do not believe that excellent qualities come from good birth. They are partly a gift from God and partly a result of good training and hard work." Suleiman mounted a fine black stallion ornamented with gold and silver, the bridle covered in pearls, turquoise and sapphires, the saddle covered in scarlet velvet. A fine horse was presented to de Busbeq. As he settled himself into the saddle he thought to himself, "What a wise man Suleiman is. He has had to bear a weight of responsibility such as no ordinary man can even imagine. A whole empire waiting for his orders, fourteen thousand janissaries and twelve thousand cavalry ready to give up their lives for him. I have heard stories of the Ottoman army camps, how ordered and quiet they are, with none of the fighting, drinking or gambling that goes on among our own western soldiers. They are used to great hardship, these janissaries. I have been told that they survive with only a small piece of canvas as a tent, and a small leather sack filled with flour, spices and salt will last them for a whole month. With it they make a kind of bread to sustain themselves. They do not question this hardship, indeed they would consider it an honour to die in the service of the Sultan. But how must it feel," de Busbeq wondered casting his eyes over the splendid Sultan on his horse, "how must it feel to hold such power?

I wonder what sorrows or regrets he carries in his heart, for he has lived and reigned long enough now to have looked back on his life and considered it well. I hope that while I am the guest of such a great ruler I will learn something of what he is as a private man."

SULEIMAN TELLS HIS STORY

THE SULTAN AND HIS ENTOURAGE RODE OUT, THE BEATERS MOVING ahead to seek out game for the hunters. Among the beautiful gardens filled with rare trees and flowers, far from the noise and bustle of the city, de Busbeq considered again what an honour it was to have been invited by the Sultan. As if guessing his thoughts, Suleiman drew his horse up close to de Busbeq and for a moment the severe mask of his face cracked with a small, fleeting smile.

"Of course, you will want to know about war," he said. "That is what every foreign ambassador wants to know about. "My strategies, my techniques and my future aims. War and my riches, that is what they all want to know about."

"Well, my lord, I know something of your riches. I have, after all, visited your palace." There was the sound of a horn ahead and Suleiman rode on, surrounded on both sides by attendants. De Busbeq slowed his horse and dropped behind. He was not interested in hunting. Speaking of the palace had brought to mind pictures of Istanbul and the beautiful Topkapi Saray. He had visited most of the famous courts of Europe and he had seen none so breathtaking.

He saw himself now, along with the other ambassadors, entering the black and white marble gateway which led into the first courtyard. The great courtyard was busy, it was filled with people, and yet it was

so quiet that the fall of a horse's hoof against the earth could be heard. There were about three thousand janissaries dressed in scarlet with their tall caps and white neckflaps. They stood so still and silent, it was as if they were sculpted from marble. Anyone could enter this court, man or woman, as long as they maintained a respectful silence. There were artists' studios for jewellers and painters and various other buildings. The group of ambassadors passed an orange grove and proceeded towards the gate which opened into the second courtyard. Just before they reached the gate they turned their eyes away from the two raised stones that stood nearby; these were stained by blood from the heads of punished officials, often displayed there as a warning to the disobedient.

The second gate was well guarded by janissaries for beyond it lay the centre of the empire, the court of the Divan where laws were made and justice carried out. Water bubbled from fountains surrounded by rare plants and flowers. Ostriches and gazelles moved peacefully among the gardens; but in the buildings that ran along the edges of the courtyard, the serious business of state was carried out. In the gold and jewel-encrusted Divan room, the Grand Vizier, second only in importance to Suleiman himself, was dressed in a long robe of white satin trimmed with sable. He administered the law of the land. He had to be very careful to be just and honest because there was a small barred window looking down on him from where the Sultan himself could listen, unobserved, whenever he pleased.

On both sides of the courtyard stood the cavalry, the *sipahis*. Every horse was a fine Arab with reins decorated in gold and silver and a bridle embroidered with crimson silk and decorated with turquoise. No, de Busbeq thought, he would not forget his visit to the palace. He would never discover what lay beyond the third gate into the final courtyard. This last gate, the Gate of Felicity, led to the private section of the palace where only the members of Suleiman's household could enter. Anyone who passed through this gate, which was guarded by twenty-five white eunuchs, kissed its threshold as a sign of respect. De Busbeq, like anyone else who came across such power and wealth, could not help being impressed by it, but he knew that there was far more to the magnificence of Suleiman than this. His wealth was only the surface; beneath the mask of ruler and leader lay a cultured and learned man who spoke many languages, had much knowledge of the world, wrote beautiful poetry and knew how to work gold into fine objects. This was the richness that he was interested in.

"So, you know something of my riches do you?" Suleiman's deep voice broke through de Busbeq's thoughts. The Sultan had shot a great stag straight through the heart and then had waited for the foreign ambassador to catch up with him. De Busbeq was startled, believing for a moment that the great Sultan had read his mind. Then he realised that Suleiman was simply continuing their conversation as if it had never been interrupted. Without waiting for de Busbeq to answer, he said. "Well then you'll probably want to know about war."

"No one ever thought that I would make a good soldier," Suleiman said and again de Busbeq noticed the flicker of a smile. "As a boy, everyone despaired of me. I was pale and looked sickly. No one believed that I would be able to rule such a vast empire. But I have proved them wrong. It is not muscle that makes a good leader of men, but courage and strategy. I was twenty-six when my father, Selim the Grim, died. I was his only surviving son and so I did not have to fight for my right to be Sultan. For this I was grateful as I did not have to carry out the terrible duty that my great-grandfather, Mehmet the Conqueror, had made law. A new Sultan's first task is to order the deaths of any surviving brothers, and I was spared this bloodshed. My name was called out from every mosque in every town of my kingdom. Fireworks lit every city with a blaze of brilliant colour and I was officially proclaimed Sultan with absolute power over all my people.

"My father, Selim, brought the Holy Cities of Mecca and Medina under our rule and made us the Protectors of the Islamic faith. I have always taken this very seriously and, although my word is law to my people, I know that I am still a servant of God. To every battle I have taken the holy relics of the Prophet Muhammad – the Banner of the Prophet and the twin-pointed sword of Ali. My soldiers know that any-one who dies under this banner will go straight to Paradise.

"From the beginning of my reign, I focused my ambitions on the West. You will forgive me for saying this," Suleiman said, turning his head towards de Busbeq, "but you Europeans seem so divided. With the struggle between Charles V of Spain and the French king, Francis I, the way seemed open to me. My targets were the city of Belgrade and, ultimately, Vienna; but first I wanted to conquer Rhodes. The Christian Knights who held the island were attacking ships carrying pilgrims to Mecca and Medina. As the Protector of Islam, I could not allow this."

Suleiman paused, and de Busbeq watched as his face seemed to melt and reform, becoming the face of a young man full of a life of its

THE OTTOMAN EMPIRE

IN THE REIGN OF

SULEIMAN THE MAGNIFICENT

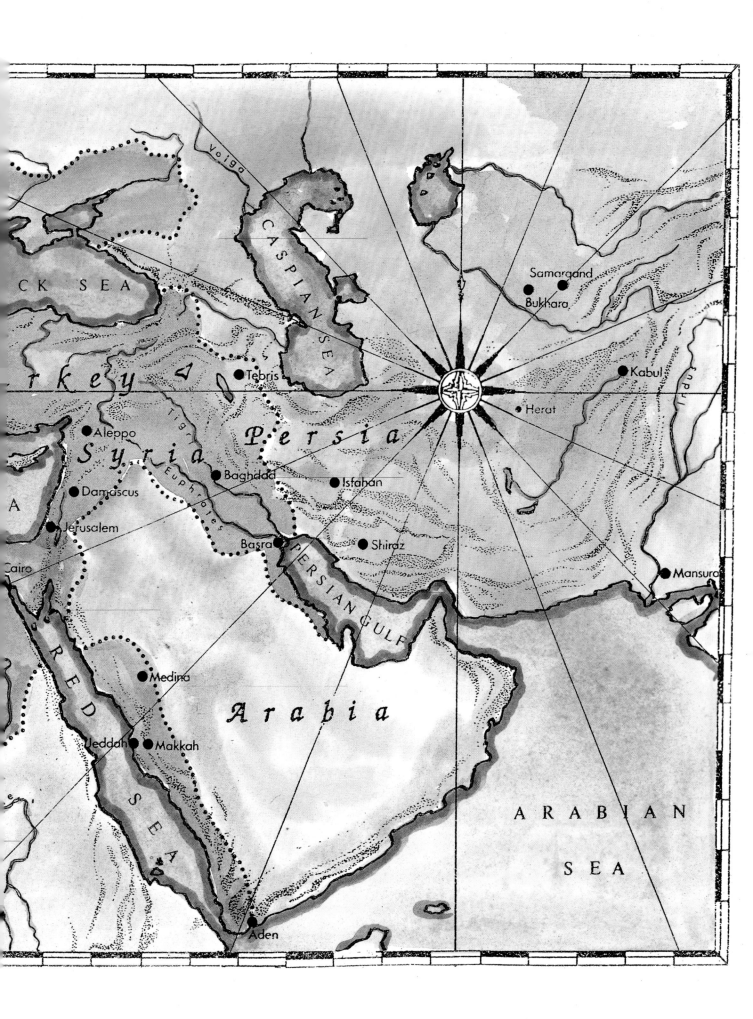

own, the blood, red with warmth under his skin, making the false rouge unnecessary. "You know," said the Sultan, and even his voice rang with new life, "war came naturally to me, just as poetry did. Of course it is cruel and destructive, but there is an excitement and energy to it that the rest of life cannot match. I cannot find the words to describe the feeling as we used to gather for battle outside our beloved city before a campaign. As a Muslim, I drink no wine, indeed I have forbidden my people to drink it, but I do not believe even large quantities of wine could fill me with the same sensations that I used to feel as I marched out to battle. The crowds prostrated themselves as I rode out of the city. They were not merely watching their Sultan setting out for war, but were witnessing the whole glorious might of the Ottoman Empire. Twelve thousand janissaries marched in front of me. The cavalry rode in groups of two thousand surrounded by banners. Three thousand gunners, and eight thousand camels, mules and horses carried our baggage. Around me were four hundred mounted bodyguards with shields on their left arms and spears in their right hands, painted green, the colour of the Prophet. The sound of drums and trumpets filled the air. Indeed, there is not an army in Europe to match us."

The Sultan's voice rang with pride, but then he noticed de Busbeq's bright eyes on him. His face became serious once more and his skin resumed its pallor. He cleared his throat. "So, I was saying that, as a young man I first set out to conquer Rhodes. The year after that I became Sultan and I called for their surrender. If they followed my orders, I promised that they would not be harmed, but if they did not I threatened to reduce the city of Rhodes to dust beneath their feet. They refused my terms so my army began its attack. The city was heavily fortified, but my men mined beneath the thick walls, digging tunnels and sinking shafts, exploding rock with gunpowder. There was fierce fighting and great loss of lives until we reached a truce. But the Knights broke that truce and from then on I showed no mercy until they agreed to absolute surrender. I believe a ruler should be generous to his enemies once they have submitted. There is nothing to be gained by needless cruelty. I met their leader, Lisle Adam, and found him to be a brave old man with many good qualities. I allowed the Knights to leave Rhodes safely and with dignity and even offered them the use of ships for transport.

"But Belgrade was the real prize. It was the gateway to Hungary and further expansion of my kingdom. My janissaries, my cavalry, surrounded the fortress and we set up our guns on an island in the River Danube. Relentlessly we bombarded the city. My ships stopped any fresh water reaching the inhabitants. It was a fierce and cruel battle. The moat was filled with the bodies of dead soldiers and heads were set on pikes along the roadsides. At last the city surrendered.

"My men look to me for leadership. I cannot show any sign of weakness or they would lose heart and I have taught myself to look at sights of horror with a calm face as if they were nothing to me. But I am a man and death and suffering does not leave me unmoved. It is indeed lonely never to be able to confide one's feelings to another human being. I was rescued from this loneliness by my beloved Roxelana. We wrote to each other during every campaign I went on. She kept my spirits up, and to her I could confess my true thoughts, knowing she would tell no one. I had absolute faith in her." Suleiman's voice had changed again; de Busbeq could not help noticing that it was filled with tenderness when he spoke of his wife. He had heard many

bad things said about her, 'that Russian woman' as she was called in the West. It was said that she held Suleiman in her power, but de Busbeq was willing to hear anything the Sultan had to say about her. He had never mentioned Roxelana to any other foreigner and de Busbeq realised that he was very honoured.

"My Khurrem, my lovely laughing one, wrote me such cheerful letters. She knew I needed to keep my spirits up. I remember once returning to my tent after a day of bloody battle and reading her letter in which she made me laugh with a story of how she had picked up a bottle of brightly coloured liquid, and believing it to be sweetened water, had drunk deeply. It was not water, but strong, bitter tasting perfume! She kept me in touch with my family, consulting me about which doctors might be able to help our son, Jahangir, who was a cripple. She was concerned with my own health and wanted me to wear a special shirt which she hoped would bring me luck and deflect any bullets that came my way. Her letters allowed me to shed, for a few private moments, the heavy robes of leadership, and it was this that kept me calm and allowed me to face battle with courage again and again."

Suleiman urged his horse forward. Into the clearing ahead, a beautiful deer appeared and turned its wide brown eyes on de Busbeq and the Sultan on their fine horses. Suleiman raised his bow and arrow, aimed, and then let his weapon drop. The deer ran, disappearing into the trees. He gave no reason for not shooting the deer, but instead spoke once again to de Busbeq riding at his side. "Will it pain you if I speak about the battles we fought with your people in Hungary and Vienna? They were cruel and hard and caused much death."

"I cannot pretend that your army is not feared in my country," de

Busbeq answered. "You conquered much land and for many years we lived in terror of the great Ottoman army. But I am pleased to say that we have reached a peaceful agreement with you. My king pays you tribute each year and you have acknowledged my presence here in your land most kindly. I wish you to speak as freely as you choose." With these words, de Busbeq bowed his head towards the Sultan.

"I was right in my judgement of this man," Suleiman thought to himself. "He is intelligent and trustworthy. I have many things I wish to say to him." For a while they rode in silence and then Suleiman spoke again.

"My campaigns in Hungary were beset with bad weather. I remember the cold, the terrible cold and the endless rain and snow. Five years after I conquered Belgrade, I recalled Ibrahim, my Grand Vizier, from Egypt where he was putting down a revolt. We planned our attack on Hungary. It took us six months of weary travel to reach the plain of Mohaçs which was to be our battlefield. To the east flowed the River Danube and in the surrounding hills, our army's reserve troops hid. The Hungarian king was young and inexperienced and was no match for us. We surrounded our enemy and destroyed them. The King himself drowned when his horse fell on him while trying to climb the bank of the river. We took no prisoners. I ordered my men to kill the two thousand that we had captured. The rain fell in torrents as I looked out on the field of destruction." De Busbeq had grown silent listening to this account. He had always known that the Ottomans were a frightening enemy. They did not look on death on the battlefield in the same way as Europeans. They considered it an honour to give up their lives.

"You think me cruel," Suleiman said, noticing de Busbeq's expression. "That is the opinion of many. It may well be true, but I do not see what good it does to sweeten the face of war. It is a brutal business, and victory did not always belong to me. When I tried to take Vienna the weather was against me. We could not break through the walls and we had to turn back after losing many of our men and horses. But come, you have heard enough about my battles and I am tired and need refreshment."

In the shade of the trees with the sweet scent of lilacs filling the air,

Suleiman and his party arranged themselves on beautiful silken rugs and soft cushions embroidered with gold and silver thread. The food was served on great golden platters. They ate from dishes of green porcelain and drank sweetened water from jewelled goblets. De Busbeq noticed that all of Suleiman's food was carefully tasted before being served to him in case it had been poisoned. The Sultan ate lightly, preferring simple food, fresh fruit, salad and bread. When he had finished, Suleiman rose and, accompanied by a few attendants, strolled among the trees. He turned and motioned for de Busbeq to follow him. He made no attempt to speak to the ambassador, and de Busbeq was unsure whether or not to break the peaceful silence. At last, speaking hesitantly, he said, "My lord, it is now quite clear to me why we in the West call you Suleiman the Magnificent, but your own people refer to you as Suleiman Kanuni, the Lawgiver. Is that not so?" Suleiman turned and looked at de Busbeq, examining his face, those bright, intelligent eyes. "He really wants to know," the Sultan thought to himself. "He is indeed superior to any other who has visited my city."

SULEIMAN THE LAWGIVER

ONCE AGAIN SULEIMAN TURNED TO HIS COMPANION. "WHOEVER IS Sultan of this great empire needs to be a good soldier." He cannot be frightened of war, or else it would not be long before he lost his kingdom. All around are people ready to nibble away like mice at its borders, taking land and cities away from the control of the Ottomans. I have had to dedicate a number of years of my reign to war, to keep the Persians, the Mamluks of Egypt and others under control. But I have not simply been concerned with conquer and destruction. When I came to power I saw many injustices and I vowed to myself that I would do something to put a stop to them. I made laws that would protect the lives, honour and property of all my subjects, whatever their religion. I taxed people fairly, according to their means. I would not allow my soldiers to take food from the peasants as they used to, instead I made them pay for it. I employed

lawyers, learned men who wrote these laws for me, laws that punished robbery and drunkenness and that forbade imprisonment without a fair trial. I wanted everyone to be able to live safely and without fear under my protection."

"You are indeed a wise ruler," de Busbeq answered. "These reforms of yours are not spoken of in the West, but I will consider it my duty to inform people of the good you have done. I think that there is much that we could learn from you." De Busbeq bowed low before Suleiman to show his respect and the Sultan gave a small nod of acknowledgement.

"I am proud of my laws," he said, "but I am even prouder of the mosques, the schools, hospitals, roads and bridges which I have built during my reign, changing the very face of my empire. I commissioned the most brilliant architect that I could find, Sinan. Together we have made a city of magnificent domes and lofty minarets standing out

against the bright blue of the sky. Nothing gives me more pleasure than attending the Friday prayers at the Suleimaniye. I set out in a great procession with two thousand janissaries on foot and my cavalry, marching in silence so that only the sound of feet and hooves can be heard. I ride with grooms walking on either side of me. In front of me are three pages, one carrying my bow and arrows, another my sword and the third the bottle of scented water that I use to wash with before I enter the mosque. All this ceremony, but the moment I enter I feel myself to be alone with God. All the jewels, colours and rich fabrics disappear. The majestic simplicity of the interior of the mosque means that there is nothing to distract me from God."

The Sultan and de Busbeq walked deeper into the gardens. Although they were followed by attendants they almost felt that they were alone with each other. De Busbeq wanted to ask the Sultan questions about his personal life, about his friendship with the Grand Vizier,

Ibrahim, that had ended so tragically; about the death of his son Mustafa and about his wife Roxelana. But he was afraid to do so. He did not want to insult the great man who had already honoured him with his conversation. His wife, Roxelana, had never been painted by anyone and her beauty could only be guessed at. During her life she had always kept herself away from the eyes of the people. To ask questions about her now, after her death, would be an intrusion. So de Busbeq remained silent. The Sultan too was silent, thinking what a pleasure it was to feel once more friendship towards an intelligent man, a man he could talk to without feeling judged. He was reminded for a moment of the wonderful friendship that he had shared with Ibrahim. Ibrahim's name had not passed his lips for years, but now he decided to tell de Busbeq about him.

"Once, walking among the gardens when I was a young prince, I heard the sound of sweet music. No mortal could play such music, I thought. It must come from heaven. But walking through the trees into a clearing, I saw a young slave boy of my age playing the violin. I spoke to him and discovered that he was not only a wonderful musician, but was also gifted at languages. He could speak Turkish, Greek, Persian, Italian and even Osmanli. He told me that he was born in Greece and that he was the son of a fisherman. He had been captured by pirates and sold as a slave in Istanbul. Ibrahim's master presented him to me as my companion and from that day on we were firm friends. We did everything together and were closer than brothers. When I became Sultan, he went on campaigns with me and I made him Governor of Egypt. I trusted him so completely that I gave my sister, Hadije, to him in marriage, so that he became a true brother. When he was only thirty years old I made him Grand Vizier, the highest position after mine. I even gave him a copy of my own ring so that he could give orders in my name as he pleased."

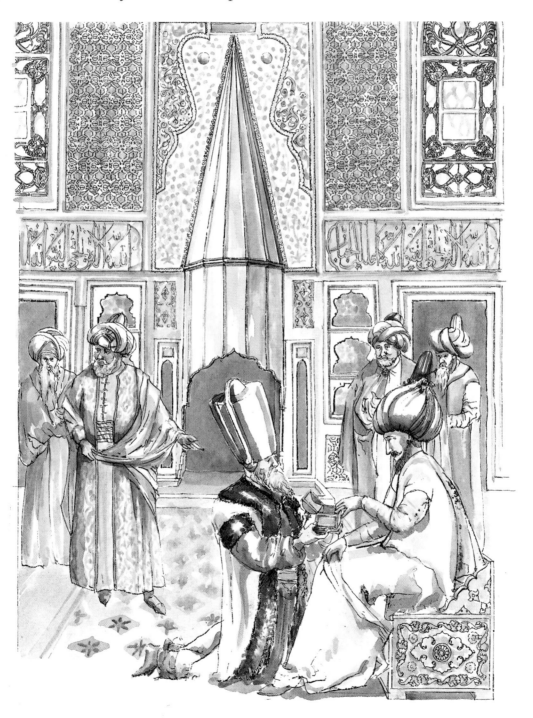

Suleiman turned to look at de Busbeq and the ambassador saw that the eyes of this great man were filled with sadness.

"Tell me what happened," he said. "Tell me what could break such a friendship."

"I began to hear bad reports about my friend. I heard that he was boasting that he was as powerful as I was, that he could make me do anything he wished. This was very bad indeed. An empire such as mine can only survive if the Sultan has complete authority. That authority must not be questioned. Ibrahim's careless words were dangerous. At first I did not believe the reports. I told myself that they were no more than malicious rumours. But then my beloved Roxelana came to me herself. Her voice ringing with anger, her eyes filled with tears, she showed me a letter which Ibrahim had signed himself using my name. He was seeking to replace me and this I could not allow. That night I invited Ibrahim to dine with me at the palace. I ate little, not wanting to share my food with someone I had once loved like a brother, but who had betrayed me. As he had so often done before, Ibrahim stayed the night at the palace. When he retired to his chamber, I gave orders for him to be strangled with a silken cord. His body was then placed outside the outer gate of the palace as a sign to everyone who passed that all the power Ibrahim had boasted of, had crumbled to dust."

De Busbeq could find no words to express his thoughts. He could only imagine how difficult it must have been for Suleiman to order the death of the man who had been his closest friend from boyhood.

"Some people blamed Roxelana," Suleiman continued, his voice heavy with sorrow. "They said that she had spread ill reports about Ibrahim because she was jealous of our friendship. But this I never believed. She was only seeking to protect me, and she was the only one who could comfort me after his death."

THE SONS OF SULEIMAN

OW THAT HE HAD BEGUN TO SPEAK OF ROXELANA, THE SULTAN'S voice lost some of its sadness. "No words could ever describe my love for her," he said. "Indeed, it would do her a great injustice even to try to speak of her beauty, intelligence and charm. Even though she has gone from this earth, no one could ever replace her and she lives on in my thoughts. She brought me great joy and presented me with the most precious gift of all, six children. Sadly two of them died while they were still very young and the youngest, Jahangir, was born a hunchback. But we loved him very dearly. I already had one son by my first wife, Gulbehar, the Spring Rose, as she was called. His name was Mustafa. A lively, intelligent boy who became a skilled soldier. I named my other sons Selim and Bayezid and my beautiful daughter I called Mihr-i-Mar.

"When my sons came of age, I planned a wonderful ceremony to

suspected nothing. But waiting for him in the shadows were four strong deaf-mutes. We use deaf men to carry out executions because they cannot be moved by any pleas for mercy. I waited behind a screen on one end of the tent. As soon as Mustafa entered, the men tried to throw a noose around his neck. But he was brave and strong and fought for his life. If he escaped he would appeal to the army to support him against me, and so I urged the killers on, while trying to shield my eyes from the terrible scene. At last they managed to hurl him to the ground and strangle him with a silken cord.

"Mustafa was much loved and many were stricken with grief at the news of his death. Jahangir, our youngest son, died of sorrow soon after he was told of his brother's death. So I lost two sons and I had to bury them. In my sorrow, I took off all my jewels, commanded that all the rich decorations be removed from the walls, and the rugs on the floors be turned upside down so that their bright colours were hidden from view. No music was played for three full days. On the funeral day I followed the coffin to the grave. The body was carried in a chariot drawn by the finest horses, in whose eyes special drops had been placed so that they would weep as they drew the bodies of my sons to their burial place.

"Then I had only two remaning sons, Selim and Bayezid. After Mustafa's death they were rivals for the throne and it was only Roxelana who could keep them from going to war with each other. When she died, I sent them to distant provinces far from one another, hoping to restore peace, but just last year war broke out between them which threatened to disrupt my whole empire. Selim had always been my beloved Roxelana's favourite and so, in her memory, I gave him my support and ordered the execution of Bayezid. Selim is now my heir and I pray to God that he will prove worthy so that all of this blood-shed will not have been in vain."

It seemed that Suleiman's face had grown deathly pale behind the layer of rouge. "So many deaths," he said. "Soon it will be my turn." De Busbeq spoke reassuring words, but Suleiman waved a hand, dismissing him. "No, no, I do not need comfort. My life has been full of triumphs. I have achieved many things and I have also suffered. But a life without sorrow is not a whole life. It is sorrow that teaches wisdom. To my dying day I will rule my kingdom as best I can, but when my hour comes, I will give myself willingly to God. Then there will be time to rest. But it has done me good to spend these hours talking to you about my life."

THE LAST YEARS

D E BUSBEQ SPENT THE NEXT YEAR IN THE GREAT CITY OF ISTANBUL. He had many further conversations with the Sultan. They learned about the customs of each other's countries and Suleiman even allowed the ambassador to read some of his own poetry which he had signed with the name 'Muhibbi' which means, 'The Affectionate One'. In Persian he wrote of his love for his wife, the burden of his responsibilities and the loneliness of old age. De Busbeq spent many happy hours in the company of the great ruler and visited the beautiful buildings that he had constructed during his lifetime. But just as their friendship was growing, de Busbeq received orders to return to his country. His king was ill and there was trouble brewing.

"I would like to present you with a gift," Suleiman told him, "as a mark of our friendship. Anything you would like. Please do not hesitate, and do not consider the cost."

"There is something," de Busbeq replied. "When I think of our friendship, I remember the scent of tulips and lilacs that filled the air as we spoke that day in the gardens. We do not have such flowers in my country and I would like to take some back and see if they might flourish in colder climates."

Suleiman smiled, and it was not a half smile, but one that lit up his whole face. De Busbeq bowed low and Suleiman presented him with his hand to kiss. They bade farewell, knowing that they would never see each other again.

When de Busbeq returned to his country, he wrote about his stay in Istanbul, about the wonderful things that he had seen and learnt. He wrote about Suleiman the Magnificent and Suleiman the Lawgiver. But he did not betray any confidences. The words of friendship he kept for himself alone.

Suleiman, although his health was failing, continued defending his kingdom. He sent his army to conquer Malta where the Christian Knights were attacking ships trading in North Africa. There was fierce fighting with heavy loss of life on both sides. Suleiman's troops were suffering from disease, lack of ammunition and food and were forced to turn back. The failure angered Suleiman. "I cannot trust any of my officers," he thought. "Only in my own hand is my sword invincible." When de Busbeq's king, Ferdinand, died and his successor refused to pay tribute to Suleiman for his share of Hungary, Suleiman decided that he would set out on another campaign, knowing that it would be his last. Old and ill, he rode in a carriage rather than on horseback.

With his army he laid seige to the town of Sziget. They surrendered, firing a salute in honour of the great Sultan and hanging the walls of their city with scarlet cloth to welcome him. But Suleiman did not live to enjoy his victory. His time had come and death claimed him.

Suleiman's Grand Vizier, Sokullu, knew what chaos would break out when it was announced that Suleiman, ruler of the Ottoman Empire was dead, so he had the Sultan's body preserved and pretended to everyone he was alive. Every morning he gave orders as if they came from Suleiman himself. Meanwhile he sent a secret message to Selim to hurry as fast as he could to Istanbul to take control. For three weeks, Suleiman's body was kept from its final resting-place. But at last he was buried with every honour in Istanbul, the queen of cities.

De Busbeq heard the news of Suleiman's death. He sat and remembered their friendship, knowing that the world had lost a great man. He would never again smell the scent of lilac without remembering the wise eyes of Suleiman the Magnificent watching him.

The Chartered Institute of Personnel and Development is the leading publisher of books and reports for personnel and training professionals, students, and all those concerned with the effective management and development of people at work. For full details of all our titles, please contact the Publishing Department:

Tel: 020 8263 3387
Fax: 020 8263 3850

E-mail: publish@cipd.co.uk

The catalogue of all CIPD titles can be viewed on the CIPD website:
www.cipd.co.uk/publications

Voices from the Boardroom

David Guest
The Management Centre, King's College, London

Zella King
The Management Centre, King's College, London

Neil Conway
**School of Management and Organizational Psychology,
Birkbeck College, London**

Jonathan Michie
**School of Management and Organizational Psychology,
Birkbeck College, London**

Maura Sheehan-Quinn
Graduate School of Management, University of Dallas

© Chartered Institute of Personnel and Development 2001

First published 2001
Reprinted 2002

Cover design by Curve
Designed and typeset by Beacon GDT
Printed in Great Britain by Short Run Press

British Library Cataloguing in Publication Data
A catalogue record for this book is available from the British Library

ISBN 0 85292 952 8

Chartered Institute of Personnel and Development,
CIPD House, Camp Road, London SW19 4UX

Tel: 020 8971 9000
Fax: 020 8263 3333
Website: www.cipd.co.uk

Incorporated by Royal Charter. Registered charity no. 1079797.

Contents

Acknowledgements

We would like to acknowledge the funding for these projects from the CIPD and from the ESRC for research on 'Workplace reorganisation, human resource management and corporate performance'. We would also like to thank Angela Baron of the CIPD for her consistent support for this research under her leadership of the CIPD's People Management and Business Performance programme, Sally Reeves for work on transcribing all the interviews, and, above all, the executives who gave up their time to be interviewed.

Foreword

This report provides the latest evidence arising from a major programme of work investigating the link between people management and business performance. Instigated by the Chartered Institute of Personnel and Development (CIPD), the overall aim of the research is to provide direction and guidance for all those concerned to maximise performance through people. The project has been guided by the hypothesis that it is possible to build reliable frameworks within which informed choices can be made about the practices that will have the most beneficial impact on performance in particular organisational circumstances.

Since first publishing evidence about the linkages in 1997, the CIPD has been focusing on three specific aims:

◻ to improve the evidence linking people management to business performance or organisational competitiveness

◻ to improve understanding about why and how people management practices influence business performance

◻ to provide accessible information on which managers can act through effective choices and decisions.

Our publications to date are:

◻ *The Impact of People Management Practices on Business Performance* (1997) by Malcolm Patterson, Michael West, Rebecca Lawthom and Steve Nickell (out of print).

◻ *The Impact of People Management Practices on Business Performance: A literature review* (1999) by Ray Richardson and Marc Thompson.

◻ *Effective People Management* (2000) by David Guest, Jonathan Michie, Maura Sheehan, Neil Conway and Melvina Metochi.

◻ *Performance through People: The new people management* (2001), a CIPD change agenda paper.

They leave us in little doubt that the link between people management and the bottom line is powerful and real. The evidence is complemented by other research programmes both here in the UK and in the USA, which demonstrate the positive linkages between practice and performance. The first section of this new report draws on findings from a groundbreaking, multi-sector, large-scale survey undertaken in the UK, jointly funded by the Economic and Social Research Council (ESRC) and the CIPD. Once again it is able to demonstrate positive performance/practice associations, albeit the data demonstrate that the link is complex and that there are marked differences in the experiences of organisations operating in different sectors.

This complexity helps to explain why, except in a small number of high-performance organisations, it is also apparent from the evidence that as yet there is limited action within organisations attributable to a real understanding of the way the performance/practice link operates.

The second half of the report deals with the views of senior managers on the contribution of people and people management and development practice in their organisations. The good news is that senior managers accept that people and the contribution they make through their knowledge, understanding of the business, willingness to be creative and commitment are the key to organisational success. They are keen to find ways to develop and manage the talent of their people better. But they struggle to develop effective actions that build on their convictions about the importance of people and enable them to apply practices in ways that maximise the contribution of their people towards business objectives and performance.

Their view of the personnel and development profession is varied, *although* the evidence from the survey data is that the presence of personnel professionals who actively implement systematic policies to manage people makes an important impact on the balance sheet. It appears that in many instances the practice of people management and development does not fulfil boardroom expectations and it is clear from this research that there are real opportunities for everyone involved with the management of people to effect real improvements in managing and developing their 'most important asset'.

The CIPD research programme is continuing and we expect it to provide further direction and guidance that will enable people managers to grasp the opportunities. What is still missing from the body of knowledge is a detailed understanding of 'what', 'why' and 'how' practices influence performance and business outcomes. This is where the CIPD is now focusing its efforts.

A two-year longitudinal study led by Professor John Purcell of Bath University is reaching its conclusion. A wealth of attitudinal data collected from a sample of almost 500 employees together with rich and varied data on organisational strategies and their implementation and outcomes over time should help us to explain many of the unanswered questions that research to date has raised.

This report is itself an important milestone and offers models and theories that will contribute to our understanding of the evidence still to come. The views of senior managers are particularly timely in helping us to ensure that the contribution of people to organisational success and effectiveness is recognised and developed as a valuable asset.

This is an evolving story that still has some way to go to reach concrete conclusions. However, the evidence is compelling and should be used to steer people management and development strategies towards meeting the expectations of business leaders and supporting everyone in organisations to make the best contribution possible to UK competitiveness and productivity.

Angela Baron

Chartered Institute of Personnel and Development

Executive summary

- This report presents further evidence on the relationship between the use of progressive human resource management and corporate performance and on how top executives perceive this relationship.

Part 1: Further evidence on human resource management and performance

- Further interim findings from an ESRC/CIPD-funded project covering a large sample of UK firms show that the average profit per employee of firms adopting up to four from a list of 18 human resource practices averaged about £1,700 in 1999–2000, compared with close to £3,400 for firms using 11 or more of the practices.

- Despite the positive trend, once background factors such as size and sector are introduced, these results fall just short of statistical significance, pointing to major differences between sectors.

- In manufacturing, the results show a strong and significant link from use of more people management practices to greater employee quality and commitment and in turn to higher profit per employee. In the service sector, this relationship is more complex and there is evidence of considerable variability within the sector.

- In manufacturing, greater use of the specific practice of job design, including teamworking, flexible job descriptions and multi-tasking, is strongly linked to higher profit per employee, although the link between use of more human resource practices and profit per employee is weaker when financial performance in the previous year has been taken into account.

- There is consistent evidence that the presence of a professional personnel specialist is associated with higher profit per employee. It appears likely that in small and medium-sized enterprises, the presence of a personnel specialist helps to bring some order, consistency and focus to personnel practice and that this pays off for the firm.

Part 2: Views from the boardroom about HRM and performance

- There is good evidence showing low adoption of progressive human resource practices across British industry. To explore why this should be so, we interviewed 48 senior executives to find out how they viewed HRM and its role in contributing to corporate performance. Three executives, typically the chief executive, the human resource director and a senior operational manager, were interviewed in each of 16 organisations representing both the public and private sectors.

- Most senior executives are, at best, only dimly aware of recent research on people management and performance. Human resource directors are most aware but do not appear to be passing this knowledge on.

- In determining human resource priorities and possible innovations, most senior executives rely heavily on their previous experience, on internal sources of ideas or sometimes on respected external colleagues of similar status. There was little reference to consultants or management gurus; a few mentioned reading, but even for them it was of secondary importance.

◘ Most executives accept that investment in people management should result in superior performance. While they generally endorse the research findings, some are generally sceptical about the research and about use of statistical evidence. By implication, even if they were aware of the research, they are unlikely to be wholly convinced by it.

◘ Executives agree that it makes sense to implement progressive people management. However, they tend to see the key to this as the quality of leadership and management rather than adoption of human resource practices.

◘ Most executives believe their organisation is already implementing progressive people management, but only up to a point. Almost all see room for further improvement. In considering this, they are more comfortable identifying improvements in specific practices such as selection, training and performance appraisal than in the HR system as a whole.

◘ The most frequently cited area for improvement is the quality of line management rather than a specific HR practice. This reflects the belief of most executives that the implementation of progressive people management is primarily the responsibility of line managers.

◘ Why don't firms do more? Several reasons are cited. One is uncertainty about *how* to do more as well as how to spot whether there is a pay-off. A second is cultural constraints, including attitudes and skills among staff. Some also cited financial constraints. An important consideration appears to be the feeling that firms are already doing quite a lot, that there is no great pressure to do more and that this is therefore not a top priority for boardroom consideration.

◘ Human resource directors are widely perceived to provide a valuable supportive role to boardroom colleagues but are not often expected to play a proactive and strategic role. Indeed initiatives from within the HR function are treated warily and viewed as often lightweight and likely to increase bureaucracy. Allied to this, there are major concerns, not least from HR directors, about the quality of personnel staff.

◘ In summary, this study indicates that those in the boardroom have limited awareness of research on people management and performance, are likely in any case to be somewhat sceptical about such research and prefer to rely much more heavily on their own experience or ideas drawn from experience within their own organisation or a few others. While endorsing the view that investment in people management might improve corporate performance, they believe they are already doing fairly well in this respect, do not see this as a top priority and also see barriers to significant improvements. Key challenges for the future include improving our understanding of what influences executives, including accessing executives' 'experience', and determining how line managers can come to accept greater responsibility for effective people management.

Introduction

There is a growing body of evidence suggesting that firms that apply progressive people management practices achieve superior performance. Much of the evidence comes from North America but there is a growing body of UK data, pointing to the same association. Among the best-known UK research is the study by a team from Sheffield University that found among a sample of mainly small manufacturing firms that HR practices had a greater impact on changes in firm performance than a range of other aspects of management, such as R&D investment or new technology. Thompson has reported a positive association between HR practices and performance in the aerospace industry. In the USA, writers such as Pfeffer have presented a persuasive business case for taking human resource management seriously. This and other research in the UK and USA has been brought together and reviewed in a CIPD publication by Richardson and Thompson.[1]

While these findings are impressive, a number of questions remain. For example, most of the UK findings are based on relatively small samples of firms in the manufacturing sector. Although there has been some work in other sectors, such as the hotel and catering industry,[2] showing broadly similar results, there is still some doubt about how far they apply across all sectors of industry. Senior managers might therefore argue that the findings are very interesting but do not apply in their sector. A second frequently raised question concerns cause and effect; perhaps it is only successful firms that can afford to introduce progressive but potentially expensive people management practices. If this were the case, there would be no reason for the less successful firms to implement them. A third question concerns the nature of human resource management and in particular what distinctive practices or combinations of practices can be included in a list that can be

described as 'progressive'. For example, one leading commentator, Pfeffer, started out with a list of about 16 practices but subsequently whittled these down to seven (Pfeffer 1994, 1998). The practices typically include extensive provision of training and development, extensive two-way communication, considerable use of teamworking and an emphasis on the design of jobs to provide scope to exercise autonomy and responsibility. However, there is less agreement about the value of providing guarantees of job security and any form of financial incentive. These issues are still extensively debated among academics and what to include is partly an as yet unresolved empirical question; but even the language can be confusing with references to a variety of terms such as 'high commitment', 'high performance', 'high road' or 'progressive' human resource management. For practitioners, the key issue is – if we wish to introduce this type of human resource management, what do we do? Is there a list of specific practices and can they be applied singly or must they be applied together, in combination, as some sort of 'bundle'?

The evidence indicates that despite the research findings, most firms have made only limited progress in introducing progressive human resource management. The authoritative Workplace Employee Relations Survey (Cully *et al* 1999) explored this issue in over 2,000 workplaces. The number of practices in place from a list of 17 core practices is summarised in Figure 1. This shows that most establishments have between five and nine of these practices in place and very few have more than 13 out of the 17.

The picture is the same at company level. The relevant results from the major survey under the auspices of the ESRC Future of Work programme and also supported by the CIPD are summarised in

Figure 1 | Number of human resource practices in place at workplace level

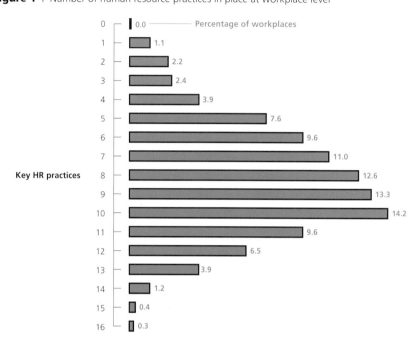

Figure 2 | Number of human resource practices in place at company level

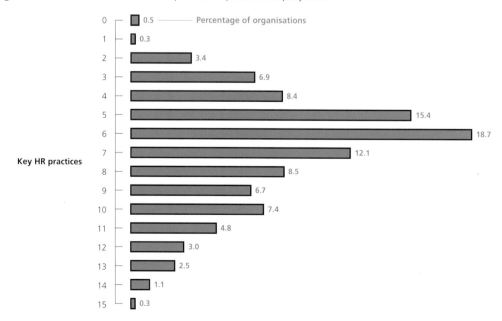

Figure 2. This again shows the number of practices in place in each company from a list of 18 core practices. This time, the typical company reports between five and eight of the 18 practices with virtually none applying more than 14 to the majority of their workforce

The findings show that at both workplace and company level, a majority of firms have no more than half the practices in place. Why should this be? If we assume that the top management of the organisation is largely responsible for this state of affairs, then we can speculate on a number of possible explanations:

◻ managers are not aware of the research

◻ managers are aware of the research but do not believe it

◻ managers do not believe the research applies to their organisation

◻ managers believe they are already implementing progressive human resource management

◻ managers are aware of the research but have other priorities that take precedence over people management issues

◻ managers are aware of and accept the research findings but do not know what practical steps to take to put them into practice

◻ a number of constraining factors outside and inside organisations lead managers to believe it is not feasible for them to implement progressive human resource management

◻ managers are deeply sceptical of fads and fashions and see human resource management as just another passing management fad that is not worth taking seriously.

The aim of this report is to address these issues. It is in two parts.

Part 1 provides further evidence on the relationship between human resource management and corporate performance. It is based on the most comprehensive UK study of company practice in this field. It covers both the manufacturing and service sectors; it explores the impact of human resource practices on performance over time, thereby addressing the issue of cause and effect; and it examines human resource practices taken as a whole but also examines the impact of specific practices. An earlier report on this study, published by the CIPD under the title *Effective People Management* (Guest *et al* 2000), reported an association between the use of more human resource practices and ratings of firm performance by human resource managers. Chief executives were also covered in the survey; they gave more weight to the effectiveness of the practices rather than their presence and reported a strong association between effective human resource practices and their ratings of firm performance. However, in both cases we had to rely on management accounts of firm performance. In the findings reported here, we have independent sales and financial data collected by Dun & Bradstreet for successive years. This gives more weight to the findings.

Part 2 of the report explores why firms do not apply progressive human resource management. It does so by interviewing chief executives, senior operational directors and human resource directors in a number of companies. The interviews explore their perceptions of human resource management and performance, their awareness of the research, their views about their current practices and their assessment of what determines their current practice. What we have, in effect, are voices from the boardroom shedding light on why firms do or do not implement progressive human resource management.

Endnotes

1 See for example the CIPD publications by Patterson *et al* (1997) and Richardson and Thompson (1999).

2 See Hoque (1999).

Part 1

Human resource management and corporate performance

David Guest

The Management Centre, King's College, London

Neil Conway

**School of Management and Organizational Psychology,
Birkbeck College, London**

Jonathan Michie

**School of Management and Organizational Psychology,
Birkbeck College, London**

Maura Sheehan-Quinn

Graduate School of Management, University of Dallas

1 | Further findings from the Future of Work study

◘ **Results show a positive association between financial performance and the use of a greater number of human resource practices across the workforce.**

◘ **In the manufacturing sector there is a strong association between human resource practices, ratings of employee quality and commitment and financial performance.**

◘ **The findings confirm the view that human resource management should be treated as a set or bundle of practices.**

◘ **There is a strong association between the presence of a personnel specialist and financial performance.**

The Future of Work study

As part of a series of studies commissioned by the Economic and Social Research Council under the broad banner of The Future of Work, a team from Birkbeck College is undertaking a major study of the relationship between human resource management and performance. Further funding from the CIPD has ensured that the study has obtained a large and comprehensive sample of firms.

Data on human resource practices, business strategy and human resource strategy, as well as management ratings of the effectiveness of human resource management, of employee attitudes and of firm performance were collected through telephone interviews in July 1999. Interviews were conducted with 610 managers responsible for human resource management and 432 CEOs. In 237 companies there were matched pairs of responses from both the head of human resource management and the chief executive. One of our main interests was to explore possible linkages between human resource management and corporate performance. Preliminary findings on some of these issues were presented in the

previous report, *Effective People Management*. The core model that informs the study, that postulates possible linkages and for which there was some support in the initial cross-sectional analysis, is set out in Figure 3.

We have now obtained sales and financial data for 409 of the organisations from Dun & Bradstreet covering the years 1996 to 1999. In this report we consider the financial results, paying particular attention to the years 1998 and 1999. In practice these often overlap into part of the following year. The assumption is that human resource practices in place by mid-1999 are likely to have an impact on the performance in the 1999–2000 financial year. Before the end of the project we will also collect data for 2000. The decision to focus on 1998 and 1999 at this stage is partly to avoid overcomplicating the results and partly because the case for going back further depends, to some extent, on whether the results for these two years alone are revealing.

The aim of this report is to present the *preliminary* and what we regard as *interim* findings on the relationship between human resource management and firm performance. They should be treated with some caution. They may be modified by expanding the number of companies for which we have financial information. Also, at this stage we have not taken into account the data on business strategy, human resource strategy or human resource effectiveness. What we are presenting, therefore, is a test of a relatively simple 'best practice' model of human resource management. This argues that it will always be better to apply more of a distinctive set of human resource practices. In this case, it is a set of what are often called 'high commitment' practices. In line with Figure 3, these are typically practices designed to ensure that employees have high levels of capability, of motivation and commitment and of autonomy and support to do the job. The assumption is that highly competent, highly motivated workers will provide superior performance and this will aggregate to higher firm performance.

The study collected data on nine main practices through a total of 48 questions. This information was collected from the human resource managers with some cross-check against selected responses from the CEOs. The practices were divided into nine groups as follows:

◘ recruitment and selection

◘ training and development

◘ appraisal

◘ financial flexibility

◘ employment security

◘ single status and harmonisation

◘ two-way communication

◘ job design

◘ quality and teamworking.

A full set of the questions is provided in the previous report (Guest *et al* 2000).

In the analysis we explore the impact of using more of these practices in combination since the logic is that they work best as some sort of bundle. However, we will also examine each of the nine main practices in turn to determine whether they have an independent impact above and beyond the others.

Dun & Bradstreet provides a range of data. The key information we used covers the size of the UK

Figure 3 | A model of possible linkages between human resource practices and corporate financial performance

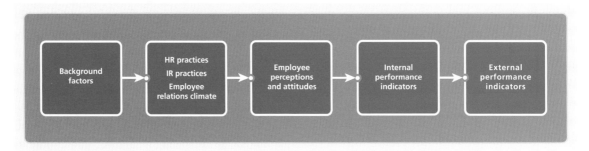

'...there is a positive but weak relationship between the number of progressive human resource practices and profit per employee...'

workforce, UK sales and UK profit or loss. From this we calculate two key ratios of sales per employee and profit per employee. The former gives a crude indication of productivity and the latter gives a better indication of employee-related profitability.

Although we have data about human resource practices from 610 companies, by mid-2001 financial data were available from Dun & Bradstreet for only 415 of them. Financial information was much less likely to be available for service sector firms. For the present analysis, we also removed firms with more than 10 per cent of their workforce located overseas. Dun & Bradstreet provides information on worldwide results for UK-based firms; we are primarily interested in human resource practices in the UK and their impact, and a large overseas operation would distort the results. Based on analysis of scatter diagrams, we identified a small number of clear outliers. These can have a large and potentially distorting impact on the results, so they were treated separately. After these adjustments, the number remaining in the main analysis was 297 for profit and 250 for sales. It is important to bear in mind that these firms represent a cross-section of British industry. Many of them are quite small and few of them are household names. So they are not the kind of organisations likely to make headlines for their innovative practices.

Human resource management and performance: the findings

The first step was to explore the relationship between the set of human resource practices and performance. We standardised the responses in each of the nine areas of human resource practice and combined them into an overall score. We started by looking at the correlation between the use of more of the progressive or high commitment human resource practices and sales per employee, which serves as an approximate measure of productivity; and profit per employee, which provides an appropriate measure of profit that takes full account of employee costs and indeed all other costs. The results show a correlation of $r = 0.11$ (sig 0.06) between the number of HR practices in place and the profit per employee and a correlation of $r = -0.01$ between number of HR practices and sales per employee. This suggests that there is a positive but weak relationship between the number of progressive human resource practices and profit per employee and no relationship between human resource practices and sales. The association between the number of HR practices and financial performance for the 297 organisations in this analysis is shown in Figure 4. (Since the results for sales per employee consistently fell short of statistical significance, we will not report them here. They are available on request from the authors.)

The information in Figure 4 indicates why the association between human resource practices and financial performance is positive but not quite significant. There is a large jump in profit per employee between those in the first and second quartiles in the number of human resource practices in place. Thereafter further increases in the number of human resource practices have little impact on profit per employee. In short, there is a non-linear relationship between increased application of human resource management and profit per employee.

The data in Figure 4 are based on quartiles – in other words on dividing the sample into four groups of equal size. The potential problem with this is that if only a few organisations are applying a large number of progressive HR practices, even in the top quartile they will get lost among others that are doing rather less. Another way of examining the data is to split the sample on the basis of the number of practices but including in the top group only those that apply a lot of the practices and in the bottom group only those that apply very few. This will provide a clearer indication of the impact of a distinctly high or low number of practices. We undertook this analysis by placing in the low group those reporting four or fewer practices in place (55 firms) and in the higher group those reporting 11 or more (23 firms). The low-medium group of those reporting five to seven practices contained 154 firms and the medium-high group, based on eight to 10 practices, contained 65 firms. For the higher group, 11 practices is still a relatively low cut-off point, but it is necessary to provide a reasonable number in the group. Even then, only 23 firms fall

into this category. The results are shown in Figure 5.

The results in Figure 5 show a much clearer association between the number of HR practices and profit per employee. In particular, they show the cost of low investment in HR and the benefits of high investment. The variation within each group and the clustering of a majority of firms in the middle categories where the differences are very small helps to explain why the results fall just short of statistical significance. But the Figure 5 pattern does confirm and help further to explain the positive albeit relatively weak association between HR practices and profit per employee in the sample as a whole.

The next step is to see whether any association between HR practices and profit emerges after

Figure 4 | The association between number of human resource practices and profit per employee based on quartiles (whole sample, n = 297)

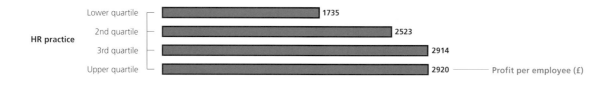

Figure 5 | The association between number of human resource practices and profit per employee based on actual number of practices (whole sample)

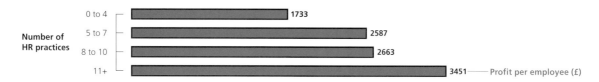

Note: The quartile analysis was based on the full set of 48 HR practices for which information was collected. The distribution in Figure 5, identifying adoption of high and low numbers of practices, is based on the list of 18 key practices, two representing each of the nine core practices covered in the survey. A count was only feasible on the basis of this list. The correlation between the two ways of presenting the HR practices is 0.92, so it is unlikely that it makes any significant difference to the results.

controlling for other factors. In this case we took into account the size of the company, the sector, a union presence and the presence of a specialist personnel manager. After controlling for these other factors, there is no discernible association between the use of a greater number of HR practices and either sales or profit per employee. However, there is a strong association between the presence of a personnel specialist and profit per employee (standardised beta is 0.22 (p< 0.01)). When we add in management ratings of employee commitment and quality, which is in line with the conceptual model on which the research is based, the results are positive with respect to financial performance, but again just fail to reach statistical significance.

Looking at the sample as a whole, the presence in the firm of a personnel specialist is associated with significantly higher profit per employee. This may indicate that people management issues are taken more seriously. Also the presence of a personnel specialist might lead to a focus on a range of basic people management concerns that were not covered in the list of high commitment practices. A further possible explanation is that in a relatively small firm, the presence of a personnel manager introduces core people management practices that move an organisation from the first to the second quartile in Figure 4.

While the timing of the collection of information on human resource practices and the financial results suggest that the practices pre-date the results, a more stringent test is to take account of the 1998 financial performance. There is a correlation of 0.67 between the financial results of firms in 1998 and 1999. While this is high, it does indicate some change. We are now in a position to determine whether HR practices are associated with any change in performance over the year

between 1998 and 1999. One of the debates about HRM and performance concerns the direction of causality. It may be that high profit enables firms to invest more in HRM. By controlling for the 1998 performance, we can be more confident that if there is still a positive association between the number of human resource practices and performance in 1999, then it is the HR practices that have led to higher performance rather than vice versa. When we control for the 1998 financial results, the influence of the presence of a personnel specialist remains a significant influence on profit per employee (standardised beta = 0.11 (p<0.05)). This is a powerful test and indicates that this is a result that we should take seriously. The presence of a personnel specialist, which in a number of the small and medium-sized firms in the sample is not something that can be taken for granted, is associated with higher levels of profit per employee (just under half the organisations in the full sample did not have a personnel specialist, based on the person who completed the interview as the senior individual responsible for human resource issues). In contrast, and contrary to the predictions in the model in Figure 3, there is no strong association between the number of progressive human resource practices and profit per employee.

The descriptive results in Figure 4 and more particularly Figure 5 appear to show the benefits of applying a larger number of progressive human resource practices across the workforce. But on the basis of the strict statistical tests, these initial results offer no clear support for a 'best practice', 'high commitment' model of human resource management across industry in general. On the other hand, they do indicate that the presence of a personnel specialist has a positive impact on profit per employee. As noted earlier, most of the UK research has been based on the manufacturing sector and it is possible that a sector-based analysis might reveal different results. In the next section, we therefore look separately at the results for the manufacturing and service sectors.

Human resource management and performance in the manufacturing sector

We undertook an identical analysis but confined the sample to manufacturing firms. This reveals a positive and significant correlation between HR practices and profit per employee of 0.17 (p<0.05). The correlation between human resource practices and sales per employee is 0.13 (p=0.13), which is not significant. The results showing the association between HR practices and financial performance in the manufacturing sector based on quartiles are summarised in Figure 6.

The pattern of associations in the manufacturing sector is similar in some respects to that for the full sample of organisations of which manufacturing is an important part. In particular, those organisations in the lower quartile with respect to the number of human resource practices also report considerably lower profit per employee. Thereafter, there is no clear linear relation between more human resource practices and higher profit per employee. The contrast with the total sample is that the top quartile appears to show rather higher levels of profit per employee than any of the others. This is shown more clearly if we look at the associations based on a distribution of the actual number of practices in place rather than the quartiles. The numbers in the four groups are 22 in the lowest group, 99 in the next, 40 in the next and 15 in the highest group. The results are shown in Figure 7.

Figure 6 | The association between human resource practices and profit per employee in the manufacturing sector based on quartiles (n = 187)

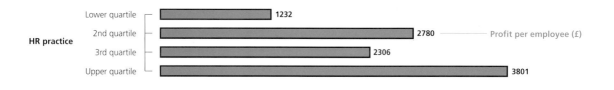

Figure 7 | The association between human resource practices and profit per employee in the manufacturing sector based on actual number of practices

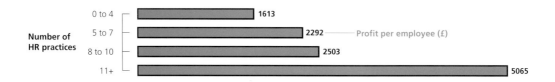

'...there is a significant association between more human resource practices and higher management estimates of employee quality and commitment.'

The results presented in Figure 7 show much more clearly the gains in the manufacturing sector from applying a high number of HR practices. The differences at the lower end are much more modest by comparison. On the other hand, the number in the group that applies a high number of HR practices is small and therefore less reliable. Despite this, the trend in the results is quite clear.

When the background factors such as size and union presence are taken into account, the direct association ceases to be significant. However, there is a significant association between more human resource practices and higher management estimates of employee quality and commitment. Employee quality and commitment are, in turn, significantly associated with higher profit per employee. The results are summarised in Figure 8.

The results in Figure 8 show a close correspondence to the conceptual model outlined in Figure 3, suggesting that 'high commitment' HR practices have an impact on employee quality and commitment that in turn have an impact on profits. The analysis in the manufacturing sector again shows that the presence of a personnel specialist is strongly associated with superior financial performance and, in this case, also with higher sales per employee (standardised beta is

0.24 (p<0.01) for profit per employee and 0.23 (p<0.05) for sales per employee). When the analysis controls for financial performance in 1998, all the results cease to be significant except for the presence of a personnel specialist that is still associated with higher profit per employee (standardised beta is 0.12 (p<.05)). What this means is that although there is some evidence supporting the model relating human resource practices to positive employee quality and commitment and these in turn to higher profit per employee, we cannot be totally confident that it is human resource practices that led to higher profit per employee rather than vice versa.

Human resource management and performance in the service sector

The analysis of the service sector firms reveals no consistent association between number of HR practices in use and profit per employee or sales per employee. The reason for the lack of statistical association can be seen more dramatically in Figure 9. This is based on the count of practices that highlights those who apply very few or a lot of the practices. The numbers in each of the groups are as follows: low (1–4) application of practices – 22; medium low (5–7) – 55; medium (8–10) – 25; high (11+) – 8. The numbers in the

Figure 8 | Linkages between human resource practices, employee quality and commitment, and profit per employee in the manufacturing sector

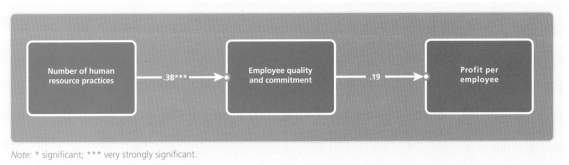

Note: * significant; *** very strongly significant.

high HRM group are extremely small so we should view their results with particular caution. In the event, it appears to make sense in the service sector to have some rather than very few practices; but the small group applying a larger number of practices report much lower levels of profit per employee. The reasons for this are unclear, but may include factors such as the composition of the service sector workforce. The numbers are small enough for it to be due to statistical error. Even allowing for these considerations, one thing these results do challenge is the contention that only firms that are highly profitable apply more HR practices.

Not surprisingly, the more complex analysis controlling for other background factors also fails to reveal any significant association. In the service sector there is also no association between the presence of a personnel specialist and higher levels of profit per employee.[1]

These results draw attention to potentially important differences between the manufacturing and service sectors. Since most of the previous UK research has focused on the manufacturing sector, they suggest that we need to pay more attention to the distinctive circumstances applying in the service sector. The results also confirm the challenge to the idea that a distinctive set of best practices is universally applicable across all sectors of industry and illustrate the potentially distorting

effect of any analysis conducted across sectors that does not clearly control for sectoral differences.

The impact of specific practices

We have seen that in the manufacturing sector there is an association between the use of more human resource practices and financial performance. The policy implications of this are potentially unclear. Given the apparent advantages of having in place a large number of practices, it may suggest that irrespective of where the emphasis lies, the more of a specific set of 'progressive' practices in place, the better. But are some practices likely to be more important than others? We examined this by looking at the impact of each practice on financial performance while controlling for all the others. In the event, in the full sample none of the individual factors had any significant association with financial performance. In the manufacturing sector, two practices had a positive association with profit per employee.[2] One was job design (the standardised beta scores for both job design and job security were 0.17 (p<0.05)), which included teamworking, flexible job descriptions and multi-tasking and which is often emphasised in the literature on human resource management. In this sample, there was generally a low use of job design practices. By implication, those few organisations that take it seriously gain some advantage. Since greater use of job design had a significant association with

Figure 9 | The association between the number of human resource practices and profit per employee based on high and low use of practices in the service sector (n = 110)

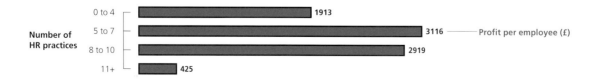

profit per employee in manufacturing even after controlling for performance in the previous year (standardised beta 0.16 (p<0.01)), this suggests that it has an important influence on corporate success. The second practice was an emphasis on job security and use of internal labour markets. The items within this factor include promotion from within whenever possible, a commitment by the organisation to employment security and no compulsory or voluntary redundancies in the past three years. They ceased to be significant after performance in the previous year was taken into account. Therefore, while a number of writers on human resource management and performance, such as Pfeffer (1998), have emphasised the importance of these issues, it is worth bearing in mind that the causal link may run from financial success to an absence of redundancies.

These results do provide some support for the role of specific practices. It is interesting to note that some of the other studies in the manufacturing sector also report an impact of job design, which tends to justify some emphasis on this practice, although wise managers might not wish to redesign jobs without taking fully into account the quality of their workforce, implying that selection and training may also merit attention.

Discussion and conclusions

This exploration of the relationship between progressive human resource management and corporate performance is based on a large sample and independent sales and financial data. It therefore offers a reasonably rigorous test. At the same time, we should bear in mind that it is a preliminary analysis and it does not take fully into account the business strategy and the market context of the firms. Nor does it consider the effectiveness of the practices. Further work on the

data set is therefore required. However, this is best conducted when the full set of financial results, including those for 2000, are all available. As emphasised at the outset, we should therefore view these results as interim and provisional. Having emphasised this point once again, what do the results tell us?

The first general point is that these results extend rather than contradict previous research. When we look at the full sample, there appears to be a positive association between the use of a greater number of human resource practices across the workforce and financial performance, defined in terms of profit per employee. On the other hand, the results fall short of the conventional tests of statistical significance, mainly because the sample includes a sizeable number of organisations from the service sector.

The second key finding is that there is an association between human resource practices, ratings of employee quality and commitment and financial performance in the manufacturing sector. We should bear in mind once again that most previous studies have tended to focus on this sector. This therefore appears to confirm earlier work conducted at Sheffield University and elsewhere and reported by the CIPD. In the full sample and to a lesser extent in manufacturing, there are indications that any association between human resource practices and profit per employee is non-linear and this may weaken the statistical associations. The first step, from very few to some practices, makes a large difference in the sample as a whole and the final step towards a coherent set of HR practices makes the main difference in the manufacturing sector. In each case the other steps where more practices are added have relatively little impact on profit per employee.

> '...this evidence confirms the view that if we are to take
> human resource management seriously, we should do so by
> treating it as a set of practices – or a bundle.'

The position is much less clear in the service sector, with less support for the generally positive pattern of results. The main reason for this is that although the pattern linking larger numbers of HR practices and higher profit per employee initially appears to be sustained, it breaks down badly when we reach the firms that have introduced a large number of practices. The number in this category is small and the findings are in stark contrast to those for the manufacturing sector, but of course, for whatever reason, financial information is less likely to be available for service sector organisations, making comparison difficult. If we break the sector down in to sub-sectors and undertake a simple correlational analysis between number of practices and financial performance in each sub-sector, it is clear that there are marked sub-sectoral differences. One implication is that we need to recognise that the service sector is much larger and more heterogeneous than manufacturing. We may need a more finely grained sectoral analysis to tease out the differences within the sector and to understand why in this initial analysis the small group of firms applying large numbers of HR practices in this sector appear to have bucked the normal trend.

Despite the modest results, this evidence confirms the view that if we are to take human resource management seriously, we should do so by treating it as a set of practices – or a bundle. The evidence from manufacturing, where firms applying a high number of practices showed dramatically superior profit per employee, confirms this. At the same time, the examination of specific practices identified two in the manufacturing sector, which had an independent association with profit per employee. These were greater use of job design and a focus on job security and internal labour markets; but even here, the causal links are uncertain and further corroboration is needed.

A third unexpected but surprisingly consistent and robust result is the association between the presence of a personnel specialist and a higher profit per employee. As we might expect, there is a correlation between size of organisation and the presence of a personnel specialist. But size is controlled for in the analysis, so the result is independent of size. It may be that the presence of a personnel specialist is an indicator of a greater concern for people management issues. It is also possible that a personnel specialist is able to focus on issues not covered in the list of high commitment practices and it is these that are having the positive impact. A further possible explanation is that in fairly small organisations, the introduction of a personnel specialist contributes to the step change from the first to second quartile in the Figures presented earlier; by implication their presence ensures that a greater number of core practices are in place. It may, of course, be no surprise to CIPD members that the presence of a personnel specialist makes a difference. However it will be a challenge to some of those who are more sceptical about the contribution made by personnel managers. This is an important point that we return to at the end of this report.

It is worth recalling that the earlier report on this study (*Effective People Management*) highlighted the judgements of managers about performance and in this context, the analysis did show an association between the use across a workforce of a greater number of human resource practices and performance. It also confirmed a link between practices and ratings of employee quality and commitment, and between these ratings and management estimates of productivity and profitability. The study also noted that despite this evidence, based on managers' own accounts, the adoption of HR practices across industry remained rather low. Certainly, few organisations managed to apply a set of practices, despite the evidence, confirmed for manufacturing in this study, that when HRM has an impact this is what makes a difference. We know too little about how senior managers, those who make policy and decide whether or not to implement human resource management, view this issue. In an attempt to shed some new light on this, the next section of the report presents the findings from interviews with senior managers from a number of organisations.

Endnotes

1 In an attempt to understand the role of human resource management in the service sector a little more fully, we examined the four sub-sectors for which we had sufficiently large numbers. These are printing and publishing (15 firms), shipping, distribution and road haulage (15 firms), food, beverage, drink and catering (25 firms) and retail (31 firms). Unfortunately we had very few firms that could be clearly identified as belonging to the financial services sector. The correlation between the number of HR practices in place and the level of profit per employee ranged from 0.17 in food, beverage, drink and catering and 0.13 in printing and publishing to –0.02 in shipping, distribution and road haulage and –0.20 in retail. None of these correlations is statistically significant, mainly because of the small sample size. However, the results are enough to highlight the diversity within the service sector. If we take these results at face value, then in the retail sector as a whole there is no competitive advantage in applying more human resource practices. But of course the retail sector is very large and most of the firms in this sector in the survey are quite small; therefore these findings are unlikely to reflect practices in firms such as Tesco that have used investment in quality of service as a route to business success. The diversity within the sector also indicates that in some parts of the service sector, a serious investment in human resource practices may be a more sensible strategy. This implies that some sort of contingency approach is required and that we need to understand more about the dynamics of each sector before dismissing human resource management as the most likely route to high performance.

2 We also looked at the association between any individual items and sales per employee. One practice, concerned with single status and harmonisation, had a significant association in both manufacturing and service sectors. This included five items concerned with standard holiday, maternity, sick leave and pension arrangements as well as shared canteen facilities and a commitment to single status. Responses were generally high suggesting that in a majority of firms these arrangements were in place. In manufacturing, greater use of single status practices was associated with higher sales per employee (beta 0.20; $p<0.05$) but in services it was associated with lower sales per employee (beta – 0.26; $p<0.05$).

Part 2

Senior executives' views on the relationship between HRM and performance

David Guest
The Management Centre, King's College, London

Zella King
The Management Centre, King's College, London

2 | Introduction

In Part 1 we suggested a number of reasons why senior managers do not implement the kind of progressive human resource practices that have been associated with high corporate performance. In this second section, we report the results of interviews with 48 chief executives and other senior managers in a range of organisations, which explore those reasons in more detail.

The objective of this research was to understand more about the limited endorsement of progressive human resource management at board level. We wanted to find out whether senior executives were aware of the research linking progressive human resource management with corporate performance, and to explore how influential that research was to their thinking and behaviour. We also wanted to explore whether senior managers think they already implement progressive HR practices, and what factors prevent them from doing so to a greater extent.

We therefore set out to answer the following questions:

◪ Are executives aware of the research findings showing links between progressive people management practices and business performance?

◪ Are executives convinced by the research findings?

◪ Do executives believe it makes sense to implement progressive people management practices?

◪ Do executives know how to implement progressive people management practices?

◪ Do executives believe they are already implementing progressive people management practices?

◪ Do executives embrace progressive people management practices as a priority?

◪ Is the implementation of progressive people management practices constrained by other factors?

◪ Are executives sceptical of human resource management departments and human resource innovations?

This report considers each of these questions in turn, and then concludes with a section linking the findings together.

Research approach

To explore these questions, we started from the premise that senior executives, and particularly CEOs, play a key role in determining HR strategy in their organisations. We therefore wanted to investigate CEOs' perceptions of people management, and their evaluations of the research evidence about a link between progressive people management practices and performance. We also wanted to investigate the perceptions of other directors, such as those at the head of operational units, often with responsibility for managing large numbers of people and who may ultimately control whether significant change in human resource management policy and practice is implemented or resisted. HR directors were included on the assumption that they play a key role in shaping human resource policy and practice. Furthermore, they may act as gatekeepers

'**...we started from the premise that senior executives, and particularly CEOs, play a key role in determining HR strategy in their organisations.**'

for new ideas about people management and they may be influential in determining how human resource management is perceived in the wider organisation. By interviewing three directors in each organisation, we had some opportunity to cross-check responses and determine the extent to which there was a shared understanding of human resource issues among important policy-makers.

In each organisation we visited we interviewed: the CEO (or managing director or equivalent), the HR director and another board-level director with significant operational responsibility. The latter group, which will be referred to as operational directors in this report, included heads of business divisions, heads of clinical directorates, finance directors, marketing directors and directors of operations. Of the 48 interviewees, 12 were female (eight HR directors, four operational directors, no CEOs).

We aimed to conduct interviews in a range of sectors, and to include public and private sectors, and both manufacturing and services companies. Sixteen organisations participated in the research, some of which were divisions or subsidiaries of larger companies. The Appendix gives brief characteristics of each of the participating organisations. Four were in the public sector, three were privately owned or partnerships, and the rest were publicly quoted. Five were manufacturing organisations. The smallest participating entity had 1,000 employees, and the largest had approximately 50,000.

Each interview lasted for approximately 45 minutes and followed a similar format. In the course of the interview we aimed to find out about the sources of executives' ideas, their evaluation of the research evidence linking people management with business performance, the extent to which

they thought progressive HR practices were implemented in their organisations, and factors constraining the implementation of such practices.

Each interview was recorded and transcribed, and each transcript was coded using NVivo software to mark extracts that answered each of the questions of interest. Then, taking each research question in turn, the sets of excerpts from all the interviewees were analysed. A simple coding frame was developed to organise responses to each question, and each excerpt was examined to identify and categorise interjections, sentences, phrases or paragraphs according to the coding frame. These may have been single words, short sentences or long paragraphs. For ease of reading, they will be referred to as *comments* in this report.

The interviews provided a rich source of information on a range of issues. In this report, we organise the responses around our attempt to understand how executives view people management, or human resource management, and its relation to business performance.

3 | Are executives aware of the research findings showing links between progressive people management practices and business performance?

☒ **Forty per cent of interviewees had none or only vague knowledge of academic research exploring the link between people management and business performance.**

To explore this first question, we simply asked our interviewees the following question: 'Are you aware of research that has been conducted by academics in the UK and USA looking at links between people management and business performance?' We also, in a separate question, asked them about the sources of their ideas about people management. Do they draw largely on their past experience for ideas, do they listen to other managers or do they learn from attending conferences or from reading newspapers, journals and books? How exposed are they to external channels for the dissemination of information about research or new ideas?

Executives' awareness of the research evidence

Figure 10 shows the distribution of responses to the question, 'Are you aware of research that has been conducted by academics in the UK and USA looking at links between people management and business performance?' Of the 48 interviewees, 12 said they were *not aware* of the research. Seven claimed to have some familiarity with it, but went on to give an *evasive answer*, talking about research that was barely connected with the question, such as McGregor's Theory X and Theory Y, or research on how groups work. Nine respondents were *vaguely aware* that such

research existed, but said they could not name it. Thirteen respondents gave a *positive answer* to affirm that they were familiar with the research. Three (all HR directors) were aware of it through their involvement with the CIPD and another HR director through conference activities.

A further seven *cited research* in their answer. One CEO mentioned Jeffrey Pfeffer's work (1998). An HR director referred to 'bundles' in her answer, implying a familiarity with the 'bundles' approach advocated by MacDuffie and others (MacDuffie 1995). One HR director referred to the Sears model that links drivers of employee satisfaction with business performance (Rucci *et al* 1998). Two other directors referred to a similar causal chain to the Sears model, although they did not mention it by name; one of these gave a detailed explanation of research by (unnamed) US academics that had informed her organisation's work on the relationship between employee satisfaction and business performance.

Figure 10 shows the distribution of these various responses between CEOs, HR directors and operational directors. It suggests that operational directors were the least aware of the research evidence, with 10 not having heard about it, or only vaguely aware. CEOs were relatively mixed, with 12 aware or vaguely aware, but only one

> '...even though HR directors may be more aware of the research, they are not communicating it to other directors.'

citing research evidence in answer to the question. As we might expect, the evidence does seem to have filtered through to the HR directors and all were at least vaguely aware of it. Seven of them gave positive answers, and four were able to cite the research evidence in their answers.

In overall terms, 19 of the 48 interviewees (40 per cent) had either not heard of the research, or gave an evasive answer. It seems that the first possible explanation for the limited uptake of progressive HR practices in the UK is partly correct: a large minority of the executives we interviewed were not aware of research linking people management with business performance. Moreover, excluding HR directors, 18 out of 32 executives (over 50 per cent) had not heard of the research. In part, this

may be due to the fact that the research findings have not been disseminated to CEOs and operational directors through channels that are accessible to them. It also implies that even though HR directors may be more aware of the research, they are not communicating it to other directors. In order to explore whether this was the case, we asked our executives about the sources of their ideas about people management.

The sources of executives' ideas about people management

Figure 11 shows the distribution of responses to the question, 'Where do you get your ideas from about how your people should be managed?' The most frequently mentioned sources were those

Figure 10 | Executives' awareness of the research evidence linking progressive human resource management to corporate performance, analysed by role of interviewee

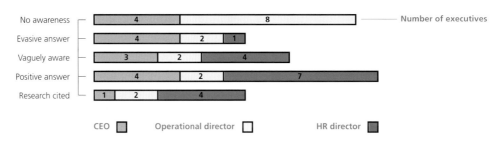

Figure 11 | Chart showing distribution of executives' responses to the question, 'Where do you get your ideas from about how people should be managed?'

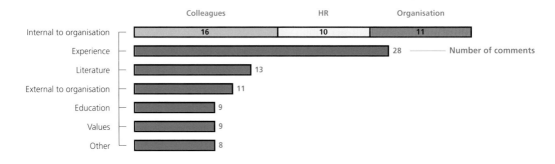

internal to the organisation, about which 37 comments were made. The top bar in Figure 11 represents these *internal sources*. It has been broken into three colours to indicate three types of internal sources: HR professionals, colleagues, and the 'organisation' or the 'business'.

Internal sources: colleagues

Sixteen references were made to colleagues, which in practice typically means senior colleagues. For example:

I get them from colleagues first and foremost. We have a style here where, to give you some idea of how it works, every week the senior team meets…and we have particular issues of policy, we knock those around together. We look to one person to take the lead in the discussion and then we try and get to a consensus view about how to handle the tricky issues of policy (CEO).

Internal sources: HR directors

Ten interviewees (six CEOs, four operational directors) mentioned *HR directors* as being a source of ideas. For example:

I would say my HR director, though, is someone who I'm close to and I will take her advice almost as a matter of principle (CEO).

I would say in hindsight many of my ideas about performance management and about what HR does and doesn't do are from the six-year period I spent in Singapore where I had a very good boss and in my mind also, a very good HR director. What I see now is that she was of a style, and now I am able to see different styles of HR director. But just the role she played, the way she played it fit very well with my boss and me at the time and I

think it is that experience that has formed my opinions, much more so than any research or business school training or anything like that (operational director).

Not all were quite so enthusiastic. One operational director commented that his ideas were very different from what he called 'HR doctrine':

So, a lot of my ideas are in some ways complementary, but in some ways diametrically opposed to a lot of the – what I would call the classical HR doctrine…I think an awful lot of HR practice is borne out of what I think of [as] command and control thinking. Command and control in the sense of central planning, that if we just plan things a little bit better and administer everything to do with the human being, all the way from performance appraisal, training, succession planning, that somehow or other the enterprise will be more successful. Now I agree with that at one level but I violently disagree with it at another. Because business is too complex to be planned in a simplistic linear way (operational director).

Internal sources: the organisation

A further 11 more euphemistic references were made to either listening to or observing *'the organisation'* or the 'business'. For example:

Largely through observing other people. Most of management is a combination of the infrastructure around you, the culture around you...and partly observation of your own and other organisations, and partly your own ideas (operational director).

I am a people watcher, so I get round the organisation, [I'm a] very high sensing, feeling, emotionally intelligent person so I watch and I feel and I learn (operational director).

Past experience

After internal sources, the most frequently mentioned source of ideas was executives' *past experience* of work, management and leadership. Twenty-eight comments were made about experience. Experience was useful because it had provided opportunities to observe tactics employed by colleagues or superiors, to see which approaches worked or didn't work, or because it had provided the opportunity to learn by doing. Experience in different organisations was a factor for five interviewees, and two mentioned the positive experience of working with people in other countries or from other cultures. In many cases, the school of 'hard knocks' had a considerable role to play:

A lot of it comes from experience. And working within an organisation where there is a tremendous opportunity to witness particular styles of leadership, particular interventions and the impact that has on people and the sort of interventions that produce positive results and get people kind of aligned with a common goal and full participants as opposed to being part participants (HR director).

Well I suppose my own personal experience, you know, the years of how have you done things right and how have you not done things right...I trained back in 1972, so I have been in the health service for almost 30 years, so you learn it by the academy of hard knocks, you know, making your own mistakes (operational director).

Literature

Another source of ideas was *literature* of some kind. Thirteen respondents mentioned this,

although only six did so as a principal source. Three commented that reading provided a subsidiary source of ideas, and two made indirect references to publications that had been influential. Literature sources included *Harvard Business Review*, the *Economist*, other business books, newspapers and industry journals. NHS Bulletins were mentioned by three interviewees, one of whom was employed in a local authority. Five respondents said that books or reading were not where they got their ideas from. One CEO said that he read HR publications, while another went out of his way to dismiss the HR press:

I like to read personnel magazines or HR magazines. Things like Harvard Business Review, *that sort of thing. My first degree was in HR, so I came out from that point of view (CEO).*

I certainly don't read the HR magazines, Managing People *(sic) – my wife does all the time but I can't bear them (CEO).*

Various external sources

Eleven interviewees mentioned *external sources*, such as client organisations, friends or contacts in other organisations, networking and conferences. Three of those who mentioned networking or conferences were HR directors. One HR director referred specifically to involvement with the CIPD as a source of ideas, although three other HR directors implied that external HR networks were not useful. Ten interviewees made some reference during the course of the interview (rather than in direct answer to the question) to academic research or to particular academics by name. Relationships with academics appear to be influential in shaping executives' ideas, even if their publications are not widely read. Interestingly,

> '...executives rely to a considerable extent on their prior experience, and on internal sources such as colleagues for ideas.'

no interviewee mentioned management consultants or other advisers, such as bankers or lawyers, as being influential.

Education

Nine references were made to *education* as being important to ideas about how people should be managed. For one interviewee, this related to education in an ethnically diverse primary school. The others referred to graduate or postgraduate studies, and one to an MBA. Three mentioned leadership and management training, including personal coaching.

Values

Nine comments were made about intuition or to personal *values* as a source of ideas about how people should be managed. People referred to a personal value base, a core set of values, a *modus operandi*, or a moral code. Two interviewees mentioned sport-related experiences, one as a professional and the other as a captain of amateur teams. Four referred to their own family background and childhood as influences on their ideas, and two mentioned parenthood.

In overall terms, these comments indicate that executives rely to a considerable extent on their prior experience, and on internal sources such as colleagues for ideas. The picture is more interesting when you consider how this differs for each role (see Figures 12, 13 and 14).

CEOs and operational directors drew predominantly on their experience and on internal sources, including HR directors. Operational directors tended to draw to a larger extent on reading, and to a lesser extent on HR colleagues

than CEOs. The picture is quite different for HR directors, who tend to rely to a larger extent on their experience than on colleagues or the organisation at large.

Initial conclusion

At the beginning of this report we suggested that one reason for the apparent limited uptake of progressive HR practices in the UK may be that senior managers are not aware of research linking them with improved business performance. Here we have seen that although many managers claim to be aware of the research, a number of their responses betrayed a rather outmoded or extremely vague view of recent developments. Only 20 were aware of the research evidence or could cite it.

Executives' limited awareness of research evidence may in part be explained by the fact that they rely heavily on internal sources for ideas. It is interesting that there was no reference made to management consultants or 'gurus' or other advisors as sources of ideas, although academics, presumably in some consultancy, advisory or perhaps educational role, were mentioned a number of times. This contrasts with some of the writing on management gurus, which suggests that senior managers are very susceptible to management fads and fashions. Our interviewees seemed to be inclined to look to colleagues, including HR colleagues and other members of the management team as well as the wider organisation. If our respondents or others like them are to be made aware of the potential impact of progressive HR practices on their organisation, this is most likely to occur via the HR directors, who have the most extensive networks and greatest prior exposure to the research evidence.

Figure 12 | Chart showing distribution of CEOs' responses to the question,
'Where do you get your ideas from about how people should be managed?'

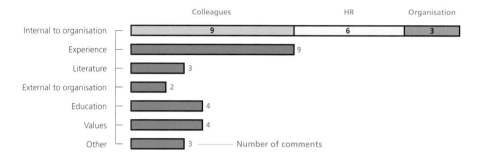

Figure 13 | Chart showing distribution of operational directors' responses to the question,
'Where do you get your ideas from about how people should be managed?'

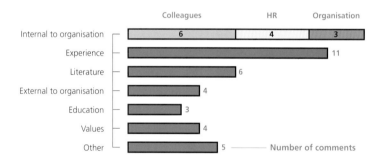

Figure 14 | Chart showing distribution of HR directors' responses to the question,
'Where do you get your ideas from about how people should be managed?'

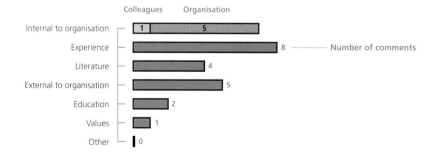

Our analysis confirms that HR directors are more likely than other directors to be aware of the research about people management and business performance. However, it seems that they have not been effective in disseminating awareness of the research evidence to their CEOs and other board-level executives. One possible reason is that the information provided by the research findings is not considered to be relevant, accessible or credible by senior executives, including HR directors. The following section explores whether that might be the case.

4 | Are executives convinced by the research findings?

◪ **Forty-five out of 48 interviewees accepted the argument that better people management would lead to better business performance.**

Having presented the research evidence linking progressive people management practices and organisational performance to our interviewees, we then asked them how credible and relevant they thought it was to their organisation. In this part of the interview, we were trying to explore whether they believed the argument that there is a link between the way people are managed and the performance of the business. We wanted to know whether executives think the evidence collected by academic researchers in support of those arguments is convincing, and whether they perceive it to be relevant to their businesses.

Here we will consider first executives' acceptance of the argument that there is a link between people management and business performance, and will then turn to their evaluation of the research evidence.

Acceptance that there is a link between people management and business performance

The argument was presented to respondents using the diagram shown in Figure 15. This diagram represents a synthesis of the findings of a number of different research projects conducted by academics in the UK and the USA. All the research represented found significant evidence of a link between people management and business performance. Consistent with the findings in the first part of this report, much of that research was conducted in the manufacturing sector.

Of the 48 interviewees, 45 agreed with the analysis implied in Figure 15, namely that greater use of progressive people management practices leads to better business performance, or said that they found it believable. Some said it conformed with their experience, while others said the analysis and links presented seemed intuitively or logically correct. For example:

All my experience would suggest that if you get it right with the people all the rest follows. You can get it right in everything else and not get it right with the people and it doesn't follow, unless you are in a highly automated situation, but even then if you don't deal with people properly during the design and commissioning phase then the automation doesn't work either. So actually, it is all about people (operational director).

Illustrating the link

Eleven executives affirmed their support for the idea that there might be a link by drawing on an example from their own or another company, or citing their own experience. For example:

I wasn't surprised by that and I don't think that is just because I am in HR because I think when I actually started off in HR I was quite cynical about this kind of thing, because if you are not careful, as I say, it comes out as – we really want you to be nice to people, because it is a good thing, you know, and you will get your reward – it sounded quasi-mystical to me really. But I actually do believe it now and I think it because, I mean I have no empirical evidence, it is simply the things you see, that when you see performance or divisions that are not performing, most of it is poor management (HR director).

> **'Of the 48 interviewees, 45 agreed...that greater use of progressive people management practices leads to better business performance...'**

I think the best example I could think of would be Halewood, which was the old Ford Escort factory...it was a terrible operation from every measurable aspect. They have converted it to a Jaguar plant, they have retrained, there is still a lot of the old labour force there, it is not like it is a greenfield site, it is a brownfield site with a lot of the old labour people in there and they are getting productivity that is better than anywhere else in the Ford world. I mean, that is proof that you can get there by human resource practices (CEO).

Explaining the link

Six executives suggested models to explain why there was a link between the management of people and the performance of their business.

It's obvious that if you manage people well your business will be more profitable. There are four levers to this business – maximising chargeable hours, turning chargeable hours into fees, turning fees into cash as quickly as possible and keeping costs to a minimum. None of those are about people. But if I don't manage people well, I won't maximise the number of hours that are worked. I will have unproductive time that I can't charge clients for. I will spend a lot on advertising and recruiting, so it's unlikely that I will keep costs down (CEO).

I think if you've got people who understand about leadership, leadership is about people management as well as clinical stuff, that should start to reduce sickness levels, make staff feel better about working here and change all of that. And it is almost linking in with the magnet hospital kind of thinking that once you are seen to be successful, people want to come and work with you, and if you end up, if it will ever happen, a

Figure 15 | Diagram presented to executives summarising the findings of academic research linking people management with business performance

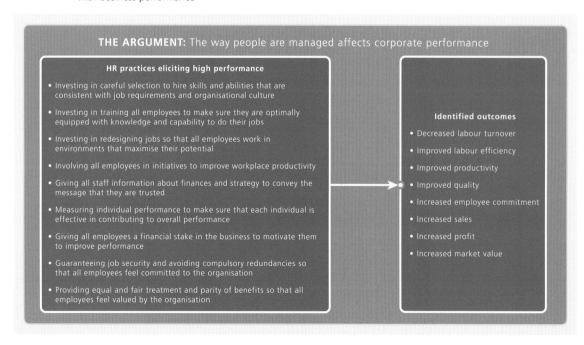

THE ARGUMENT: The way people are managed affects corporate performance

HR practices eliciting high performance

- Investing in careful selection to hire skills and abilities that are consistent with job requirements and organisational culture
- Investing in training all employees to make sure they are optimally equipped with knowledge and capability to do their jobs
- Investing in redesigning jobs so that all employees work in environments that maximise their potential
- Involving all employees in initiatives to improve workplace productivity
- Giving all staff information about finances and strategy to convey the message that they are trusted
- Measuring individual performance to make sure that each individual is effective in contributing to overall performance
- Giving all employees a financial stake in the business to motivate them to improve performance
- Guaranteeing job security and avoiding compulsory redundancies so that all employees feel committed to the organisation
- Providing equal and fair treatment and parity of benefits so that all employees feel valued by the organisation

Identified outcomes

- Decreased labour turnover
- Improved labour efficiency
- Improved productivity
- Improved quality
- Increased employee commitment
- Increased sales
- Increased profit
- Increased market value

waiting list for vacancies, then your outputs are so much better because your sickness levels go down, morale goes up, turnover goes down, patient throughput increases, mortality, morbidity decreases as well (operational director).

Eight respondents said that this was something they were convinced about personally, and that they were trying to convince other members of the management team. For example:

I think this is an area where executives need to devote more and more time – it is the bit where you can really make a difference, and I think it is the unique selling point of the business that if you are truly motivating and developing your people and they have an absolute clear focus on where the business is going, that is the real competitive advantage (HR director).

Experience of the link

Eleven interviewees gave concrete accounts of how investing in HR practices had had an impact on their organisation, or in two cases, a previous organisation that they had been involved with (both of these were reasonably new to the job). The most striking story came from a CEO, HR director and operational director from the same NHS trust, who gave consistent accounts of the impact of HR practices and cohesive leadership on their organisation. In the first excerpt, the HR director describes the situation when he first arrived in the organisation, five years ago. The story is then taken up by the CEO:

And we identified part of the transformation to the programme undertaken here five to six years ago and identified a number of major fault lines in the way the hospital was performing, doing service. [We identified that these] weren't trivial to

the adequacy in the way we managed our human resources here and identified a number of strategic changes which we needed to make in order to remedy that. So that gave us a sort of strong, and fairly objective assessment on what the problems were and why we had to start to pay much more attention to things like appraisal, the way we've managed our staff, the way we've managed to change in the organisation, that we were – our whole service capability was entirely dependent on our ability to recruit and attract and retain staff – and lots of things going against us to why people would not find this a particularly attractive place to come and work and therefore we had to work particularly hard to remedy that. Or we wouldn't be able to deliver the service required of us (HR director).

This past year we've improved our retention rates [of nurses] by about 5 per cent – so it was about 20 per cent. [That has been achieved through] staff development programmes, delivering what we say we will deliver, [introducing] flexible working hours. Looking at time out for them to actually get a breather rather than a hard slog. We have counselling, mentor systems. The induction programmes are fairly lengthy so that people actually feel confident when they are set free and I think that all those things add up to people feeling comfortable. I think these changes are being reflected [in the performance of the organisation]. At the moment I am not hearing any screams of anguish from any department and yet we are unbelievably busy. In the last year we have had an increase by 26 per cent in emergency admissions, we've had 20 per cent increase in paediatric emergency admissions and 14 per cent in adult, 23 per cent increase in over age 75 in terms of those emergency admissions and yet we are still meeting the targets in terms of our elective waiting list procedures and so on – now that is a lot of hard work. Length of stay, dependency complexity – I think that is quite important and yet the morale is good so I think that that actually shows that something is going right somewhere (CEO).

Putting the link into perspective

In overall terms, almost all the interviewees found the argument that progressive people management leads to better business performance, presented in Figure 15, to be credible. (The perspective of those who did not is described in Chapter 5). However, we should note that 10 interviewees commented that the HR practices identified on the left-hand side of Figure 15 were only part of the answer to achieving the outcomes on the right-hand side. Many other factors also affect business performance. For example:

I subscribe to this as a general proposition. I think when you come down to the specifics I think one would question whether the – I note that you just have one arrow which implies that ummh, you know it is difficult to identify specifically one thing – and say that has a specific issue on that. You may be able to do that if you looked at it in some detail. I subscribe to that proposition, I think it is a very broad aspect and it is part of a wider range of issues that do affect corporate performance (HR director).

So the difficulty about measuring, and this is one of the problems with this whole area, is it becomes very hard to demonstrate that one set of things made that much of a difference, although you instinctively feel that it does (operational director).

Executives' evaluation of the research evidence

Having explained the arguments made about links between people management and business performance, we then introduced two other diagrams showing evidence from two studies conducted in the UK. One of these diagrams (Figure 16) showed preliminary findings from the manufacturing companies in the Future of Work study described in Part 1 of this report. The second diagram showed some earlier findings from research conducted in 67 single-site manufacturing companies in the UK by Sheffield University (Figure 17) (Patterson *et al* 1997). It suggests that improvements in profitability and productivity over a three-year period were explained to a larger extent by HR practices than by other factors such as investment in R&D, business strategy or the use of advanced technologies. In each case we were careful to explain the background to the research, and to clarify the significance of the figures presented.

The value of measurement

Thirteen interviewees (eight of them HR directors) welcomed the attempt to measure the contribution of HR practices, or to provide metrics to support arguments that they personally endorsed:

If you can prove stuff and you can demonstrate stuff then it is much better and I think if people know you can do that you get a better chance of getting things done, and not really because I am necessarily that interested in the results of the

Figure 16 | Diagram presented to executives showing evidence from the Future of Work project linking people management with business performance

THE EVIDENCE (1): Profit per employee increases with increasing HR commitment

Source: ESRC Future of Work project conducted by Birkbeck College, London 1999.

Figure 17 | Diagram presented to executives showing evidence from the Sheffield University research linking people management with business performance

THE EVIDENCE (2): HR practices account for 17% of performance improvement

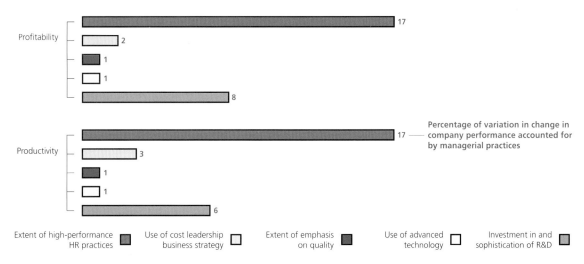

Source: 67 UK manufacturing organisations; research conducted by Sheffield University, 1997.

> **'One questioned the use of profit per employee as measure of an organisation's commitment to its human resources, on the basis that you could boost profit per employee by making redundancies.'**

measures but because I am pretty sure that if we are managing the staff effectively we are going to get more productivity. I don't really feel the need to test that – I am pretty convinced that is going to be the answer, but I think it is a very useful tool in getting it implemented (CEO).

What we need to be able to do is to demonstrate that the changes in the way we actually employ people actually do flow through to changes in the bottom line. If we could do that then they [senior management team] would take this entire [HR] function a damn sight more seriously than has historically been the case (HR director).

A few interviewees were unfamiliar with the use of statistics to present data and two were sceptical about the use of statistics to make arguments. One questioned the use of profit per employee as measure of an organisation's commitment to its human resources, on the basis that you could boost profit per employee by making redundancies. Five questioned the implied causal track of Figure 16, arguing that companies with higher profit per employee would be more likely to spend money on HR practices.

Problems of interpretation

A number of interviewees found the Sheffield data (Figure 17) difficult to interpret or were bemused by the findings. One CEO from a services organisation thought they seemed credible, while another director (also from a services organisation) wasn't so sure:

Well I am not really surprised, especially in manufacturing where I mean, these people really pay attention and are motivated, for instance the quality of what they do is – you can see it physically (CEO).

It also depends on the base you started at, doesn't it, in terms of increases [in] the profitability. There are certain things you could see, like advanced use of IT could make people a lot more productive. As a one-off maybe. Whereas high-performance HR practices, that must involve a continuing programme. Is it possible – yes. Do I recognise the shape of the graphs – no, not really. Are they feasible – yes. Are they correct – I don't know (operational director).

Several executives made suggestions about why the Sheffield findings come out so strikingly in favour of HR practices, rather than the other factors. They argued that employees' discretionary effort, elicited by high-performance HR practices, is significant in a manufacturing context because human resources can leverage the impact of other resources. For example:

But if you think about it, if you take any business now, in the world, availability of capital is a universal commodity, the price of capital is a pretty universal commodity. The equipment that people use is a universal commodity. The technology and the knowledge is almost becoming universally available. So what is the only thing you have got in your business that is unique to your business, that's the people who are within it. So somehow or other, you have to put those ingredients together in a way that leverages and creates something that is more successful and people are at the end of it because at the end of the day people do business with people and that is what we are all about. We are not about machines engaging machines, once you've done that, that is a strictly one-off thing. But in order that you have a completely adaptive system which is what business really is at the end of the day then it is all about people, so getting people to have the right behaviours, the right values and the right processes to achieve whatever they are trying to achieve, that is the thing that differentiates the winners from the losers, in my view (operational director).

However, one executive from a manufacturing organisation argued that the relationship between HR practices and business performance was not as simple as implied by the Sheffield research, since if you were in a business with a high rate of product change, investment in R&D would be far more important than HR practices. A CEO from another manufacturing organisation thought it was dangerous to draw generalised conclusions from one specific piece of research.

Relevance to their business

Interviewees were divided over whether the evidence presented to them was relevant to their business. When asked, 11 respondents from the service sector thought evidence from manufacturing organisations nonetheless relevant to them. They argued that the discretionary effort of employees is even more important in a labour-intensive context than in manufacturing. For example:

It is more relevant here. The reason I work in the health service is because it is so labour intensive. I used to work for [an industrial organisation] where I think we actually had far less impact. Even though the impact was great, the impact in a labour-intensive organisation like this you can change the world if you get your HR practices right (HR director).

Yes if anything I would expect [the contribution of HR practices to profitability] to be higher in a services company because much more of your expenditure is so marginal – small percentage

improvement in the performance of one resource, if that is a very big resource, if the salaries and benefits constitutes 80 per cent of your expenditure, then a 10 per cent improvement in the productivity of that sector is going to do more to the bottom line than if you've got people who are really only a tenth or a third of your operating costs (CEO).

No, it is relevant. I have probably seen published articles that say similar things based on this, but that doesn't hold any surprises for me and I wouldn't have thought there was much difference actually, whether you are managing Heinz Baked Beans or a social care organisation. If you invest in staff your productivity, whether it is profit or quality of services, it has got a better chance of being a higher and acceptable quality (operational director).

One CEO from a manufacturing company also thought the evidence was relevant and believable, although he could not comment on the quantum of the findings. Two executives from the same organisation expressed caution in applying the results, suggesting that their relevance depends on the nature of the industry. Five executives from services organisations also commented that the findings were not relevant to them. Four of these were HR directors, who said that they would find it hard to present the evidence to their colleagues unless it related to organisations similar to their own. A fifth executive argued that a link between HR practices and business performance was not necessarily evident in investment banking:

My push-back on that might be that our industry might be different, and the reason I say that is that two of the most profitable investment banks in the world are Goldman Sachs and Morgan Stanley and they do not promote friendly, cuddly HR services –

'...it seems that senior executives do endorse the idea that investment in progressive people management practices should result in improved business performance.'

they don't. This point is not something that worries them at all (operational director).

Initial conclusion

At the beginning of this report we suggested that one explanation for the limited uptake of progressive HR practices in the UK is that executives may be aware of the findings but not believe them. In this study we presented the findings to them and sought their evaluation of them. With only three exceptions, all accepted the broad arguments that were presented. Thus it seems that senior executives do endorse the idea that investment in progressive people management practices should result in improved business performance. However, concerns were raised by a fifth of them about making claims about the impact of HR practices in isolation from the raft of other factors that affect business performance. Also, as we shall see later, many were uncertain about how to go about implementing progressive people management practices, even if they acknowledged their importance.

A good deal of scepticism was expressed about the research evidence. While almost a quarter of our interviewees welcomed the use of quantitative methods to evaluate the contribution of HR, a similar number were confused by or uncertain about the use of statistics to support this kind of argument. There was no clear consensus about whether findings from manufacturing companies (which appear to be more persuasive on the basis of our findings and other research) might be applicable to other industries or sectors.

Our analysis suggests that it is unlikely that the research would be influential in shaping thinking and behaviour, even if research findings were better disseminated among senior executives. They seemed more likely to accept a link between progressive people management and business performance on the basis of their experience, their values or what they learn and observe informally from others than on the basis of research evidence, however well that research may be conducted and however convincing the results. Despite the failure of research evidence alone to convince senior managers, they may nonetheless act on their belief that effective people management is important. In the following section we explore whether our interviewees thought it makes sense to implement progressive people management practices.

5 | Do executives believe it makes sense to implement progressive people management practices?

◪ **Selection and performance management were the practices most commonly thought to have an impact on business performance.**

We saw in the previous section that almost all of our interviewees endorsed the argument that there is a link between people management and business performance. Thus we might be led to infer that executives think the implementation of progressive HRM is worthwhile. However, if we look in more detail at some of the comments made about the research evidence, and particularly those relating to specific HR practices listed in Figure 15 (see page 28), we see that a more complex picture emerges.

Challenging the case for implementing progressive people management

The importance of context

Two of the executives we talked to questioned whether the implementation of progressive HRM was worthwhile. The first speaker below argued that while this logic might be applicable to an expanding business, the parlous state of his industry was such that investing in people could not be seen as a means to boost organisational performance. The second was hesitant about endorsing the suggested relationship, feeling that it was almost politically correct to do so:

I think in a different organisation I could be persuaded [that investing in HR practices would have an impact on business performance]. I think in this organisation with the market pressures and the knowledge that in a year's time there will be less people in the business than there is today and in two years' time there'll be less again, umm,

making a justification for that is hard…whereas if we were a static business in a static market or preferably in a growing one, then I would find it much, much easier to accept the argument I think. With both cash pressure, profit pressure, and the number of people reducing, I find that a bit hard (operational director).

I think it, the reason I am hesitant and dodging around a bit, is because I think it would be too easy to say 'yes' and I'm not sure that that is accurate…It is hard to fall out with any one of those individual statements and there is almost a politically correct – yes, I've got to say yes to that and therefore it equals that and therefore it equals that. And there is a bit of me which intuitively is saying, hold on a minute that's not right (CEO).

The importance of good leadership and management

A third executive (an HR director) objected to the assertion that HR practices, rather than the quality of leadership or management, can somehow account for business performance. This is a theme that we will return to further on in the report:

Well at the risk of making myself extremely unpopular, you see that's, that is what I am talking about. You see to me I read [Figure 15] and I say, well but that is sort of, that is just – any first, second line supervisor, manager would know that those are all the sort of common sense principles about managing people so why do we have to create some special edifice (HR director).

> '...four...interviewees...endorsed the idea that there is a link between HRM and business performance but questioned whether the implementation of progressive HR practices was strictly necessary.'

The language used by these respondents (such as 'dodging about' and 'unpopular') is interesting; it suggests a degree of discomfort in disagreeing with the arguments presented. The HR director's criticisms were echoed by four other interviewees, who endorsed the idea that there is a link between HRM and business performance but questioned whether the implementation of progressive HR practices was strictly necessary. They argued that it is the quality of management and leadership that makes the difference. If people are managed well, the outcomes on the right-hand side of Figure 15 follow naturally, irrespective of the state of HR policy and practice. For example:

Are all those combinations together going to guarantee that if you did every one of them you would have a successful business, no, because again it would depend a great deal on the guy that was at the top of it. And the team that he has got around him. So you could do all the right things and still not get the results, if you had the wrong people (CEO).

Two interviewees extended this argument by asserting that it is impossible to separate HR practices from business management:

I think there is a danger of getting mixed up – are we talking about HR practices, are we talking about HR departments, who is carrying out the HR practices? That is where it gets a bit confusing. Because you could actually have quite good HR practices which are kind of embedded in an organisation just through habit and have a pretty crummy HR department (HR director).

I guess I would come back to where I started that I don't actually regard HR practices as separable from business management and I think anything that tries to correlate good HR functions and the

positioning of HR functions in organisations with business performance is almost doomed to be praying in aid of those functions (operational director).

Alternative approaches

One interviewee acknowledged that progressive HR practices might have an impact on business performance, but argued that there are other approaches, such as encouraging employees to 'work themselves into an early grave', which might ultimately be more profitable for the organisation:

There is no doubt in my mind that if you do invest in your staff you are likely to – you know, put more in you get more out, simplistically...the conundrum I have is not, is there a logical link, I'm sure there is, the question is which is the more sustainable or better approach and do you just do it in a financial way and say, look, I'll give you buckets of money if you work yourself into an early grave, or do you do it other ways (operational director).

Thus it seems that even when they acknowledge a link, many executives are not necessarily convinced about the need to implement progressive HR practices. Some extended the argument that good management is more important than good HR practices. Though it may appear semantic, some managers were more willing to endorse the importance of effective management of people than of effective people (ie HR) management. In other words, the task is one of general management rather than confined to the domain of HR specialists. Moreover, if we look in more detail at some of the comments made about whether they would expect to see a link between specific HR practices and business performance, we find that they are more convinced about some HR practices than others.

Voices from the Boardroom | **37**

Do executives believe it makes sense to implement progressive people management practices?

The link between specific practices and business performance

During the interviews, 74 comments were made by our interviewees about specific items in the list of human resource practices in Figure 15 and their impact on business performance. These emerged from a general request to comment on the model and the practices listed. Figure 18 shows the frequency and distribution of these comments. Some interviewees endorsed the idea that specific practices might improve business performance (these comments are represented in the upper half of Figure 18), and some questioned whether certain practices would have an effect on business performance (these are shown in the lower half of Figure 18). Almost half of the comments (36) questioned whether a positive impact would be seen.

Favoured practices

Figure 18 indicates that *selection* and *performance management* were the practices most commonly mentioned as likely to have a positive impact on business performance, although performance management was often defined quite narrowly in terms of performance appraisal. No one suggested that either of these was likely to have a negative impact. Three interviewees explained the importance of selection in terms of the cost of trying to correct poor selection decisions, and two CEOs argued that selecting people who fit with the organisational culture was key. The following quotes give examples of the expected impact of these two types of practice:

The hiring is very important and it is the first step. If you make mistakes in hiring people then you pay, and it is a painful process (CEO).

Figure 18 | Distribution of executives' comments about whether they would expect to see a link between specific HR practices and organisational performance

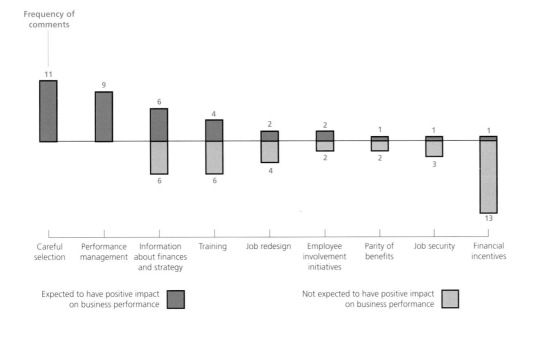

> **'One concern raised was that the link with the share price of the overall business was too distant from decisions made by the average employee.'**

'Measuring individual performance to make sure each individual is effective.' Well that is absolutely vital to our business, probably more vital than any other of the points, because they are such high-performance individuals it is very important to have an accurate assessment of how well they have done. Even more important than that though is they all think that they have performed better than anybody else so they want to make sure that you have a very good appraisal system of marking everybody else. So they are not so selfish to think, I'm the guy whose done everything. But they are selfish enough – not so much selfish, just realistic – to think, I'm working bloody hard in this business, I do not want to be carrying anyone (operational director).

Six interviewees said they would expect *sharing information* about finances and strategy with employees to have a positive impact on firm performance, and six others raised concerns about this. Three observed that staff want to feel they are included but ultimately are not that interested in the content of such information. Others questioned whether information about strategy would be understood by employees, or drew attention to the dangers of making such information widely available.

Questioned practices

Of the four respondents who made comments about links between *employee involvement* and organisational performance, two supported the idea that there might be a link. Two respondents in professional services organisations thought it would not be productive or feasible to invite ideas from the whole workforce. Three comments were made about links between *parity of benefits* and organisational performance. One CEO agreed that top managers should not feel they are 'above the

law'. Two interviewees questioned whether there would be a link: one (from a professional services firm) acknowledged that providing equal opportunities was a desirable goal, but argued that ultimately it was more important to focus on and develop the 'really capable people'.

Challenged practices

On balance, executives were more often negative than positive about the role of *training* and of *job design*, which are often viewed as core elements of progressive or high-performance people management. These views are revealing in the context of findings in Part 1 of this report, which reveal that in the manufacturing sector job design is the one practice that shows a strong causal link to higher profit per employee. *Giving employees a financial stake* was the area where executives were least convinced about possible benefits in terms of organisational performance. As Figure 18 shows, only one interviewee expected it to have a positive impact, commenting that he thought it would reduce turnover at managerial levels. Thirteen executives did not think employee share ownership would necessarily have a positive impact. One concern raised was that the link with the share price of the overall business was too distant from decisions made by the average employee. Another was that the upside came to be expected or taken for granted:

'Giving all employees a financial stake in the business' – yes it's a given and bits of that are happening. Although again even in our industry it doesn't really motivate them, the reason it doesn't really motivate them is on balance if it's shares, they either go up or go down, if they go up they just take it as given, if they go down they get really depressed. So it is not a zero sum game, on balance you wonder – I wonder if it would be

better if we didn't do it. The second element of this is often these shares are meant to retain them, and they don't (operational director).

I am not a believer in just splashing equity and financial stuff at people because if they don't understand it and they don't think they can affect it, how the hell can it motivate them (CEO).

Thus, in overall terms, it seems that interviewees were more convinced about the impact of careful selection and effective performance management on corporate performance than they were about giving employees a financial stake in the business, training them, redesigning jobs or providing job security. Opinions were divided over giving employees information about finance and strategy and employee involvement initiatives, while executives on balance were sceptical about the benefits for organisational performance of training, job redesign and providing a financial stake in the company.

Initial conclusion

We saw earlier that most executives accept the idea that there might be a link between the way people are managed and business performance. However, this section provides an interesting counterpoint. It is almost as if executives feel obliged to ratify the argument that people management affects business performance. Despite considerable effort made by the interviewers to present the evidence in an unbiased manner, and to invite objective comment, the defensive language used by some of the respondents suggests that they felt some kind of pressure to offer a confirmative answer. This difficulty was expressed by one interviewee:

I would have great difficulty in saying that this isn't anything other than very sensible and realistic, which isn't quite the answer you are asking for, because there is a shopping list of 10 items [in Figure 15] which if every one of them were done it would be pretty bizarre if we didn't get [improved business performance] (CEO).

One reason for this discomfort is perhaps that executives think the link between people management and business performance operates as much through the quality of management and leadership as it does through the implementation of HR practices. Progressive HR practices are not, it seems, the whole answer. Again the emphasis is as much if not more on effective management of people as on effective people management.

Moreover, a significant proportion of our interviewees were sceptical about the benefits of implementing the full range of practices listed in Figure 15. They were more convinced about the benefits of individualised practices (such as careful selection and performance management) than they were about more involvement-orientated and collective practices (such as employee involvement and giving a financial stake in the business).

This is interesting in the context of broader arguments about high-performance work systems. Proponents of the benefits of HR practices argue that such practices need to be implemented in a coherent, interlinked and mutually supporting manner. To secure the full benefit, it is argued that a 'high performance' work system needs to be in place, where employees operate in a high-trust, high-involvement environment where their discretionary effort makes the difference to the organisation's bottom line. Here, in contrast, our respondents seemed to be more impressed by policies and procedures aimed at making individuals more motivated and efficient, rather than those intended to invoke a collective effort toward improvement. Thus, while they endorse the importance of managing people well at an overall level, they do not necessarily accept that a set of 'high-performance HR practices' and the model set out in Figure 15 are the best means to achieve this.

6 | Do executives know how to implement progressive people management practices?

◨ **Twenty-nine out of 48 (60 per cent) interviewees commented on the difficulty of implementing progressive HR practices effectively.**

Another possible explanation for the lack of uptake of progressive HR practices in UK organisations is that executives accept that it is important but do not know *how* to go about doing it. To explore this, we will return to some of the comments made by executives when evaluating the argument that there is a link between HR and business performance (shown in Figure 15 on page 28) and also consider reasons cited for not investing more in human resources.

The general question of how to implement progressive people management

When presented with Figure 15, nine interviewees (three CEOs, two operational directors, four HR directors) said that, while they did not dispute the importance of implementing some of the HR practices, the more important question was *how* they were implemented. For example:

What it doesn't tell me on this particular sheet is what you are defining as excellent HR practices…the key to it of course is, well a company may say yes we are investing in careful selection to hire skills and abilities, but what does careful selection mean?…The issue for us is, in this particular industry at this stage of the business cycle are some of these more important than others and by the way, what is it that you do to have careful selection and hire skills? What sort of training should we have? (HR director).

A lot of what we need to do, I wouldn't say [is] obvious, but it is not really disputed. You put a list

of HR practices in front of me and I'll look at them and say would I like to do most of the things, yeah. It is not that there is a great deal of debate about what would be a good idea – whether it would be a good idea to work with the staff to get more out of them and get more for the business, and provide them with a better environment – all these types of things. The challenge is how do we actually do it (CEO).

How much investment in HR? Is more always better?

Another criticism, raised by seven respondents, was a question of how much of the HR practices listed on the left-hand side of Figure 15 should be done. A minimum is clearly important, but how much effort, resources and time should be spent upon these HR practices?

And investing in training all employees to make sure they are all optimally equipped with knowledge and capability. Well, it would be a nutcase who said that can't be right. I can't, what I can't argue very accurately is how far along the continuum we need to go…I think what I am trying to signal up is that there are subtleties within each of them, that the bald statement feels right but if you think of it on a sort of continuum then how far down the continuum do you go…I am not convinced that I have to go all the way down the continuum (CEO).

I think that there must be diminishing returns…how carefully can you go about

42 | **Voices from the Boardroom**

Do executives know how to implement progressive people management practices?

> '**While they recognised that investment in people management is important, another group of executives were uncertain about how much of a return they could expect to see.'**

recruitment, for heaven's sake, we do it to the nth degree, there comes a point when you can't go any further (operational director).

Three turned the argument around, claiming that HR practices were 'hygiene factors' that you had to get right at a minimum, but that cumulative investment in them wouldn't necessarily deliver proportional returns in terms of the outcomes listed. These arguments suggest that there is some doubt about the implied linear relationship between investing in HR practices and business outcomes. While they recognised that investment in people management is important, another group of executives were uncertain about how much of a return they could expect to see. Ten interviewees talked about the difficulty of knowing how to quantify or assess the benefits of such programmes:

When we are doing planning in terms of numbers we can all agree on a number very quickly but when it is what do you want out of your people and how are you going to measure it then that is much more challenging, and even agreeing – actually the first part is quite easy – this is what we would like our people to do, but how do you measure it and how do you know you are going in the right direction (HR director).

I think with so many of these initiatives it is difficult to identify where the benefits really have been achieved...Developing your people, giving them a leadership development programme, very, very difficult then to show, or to find a measure that would demonstrate that the investment of £0.5m has actually produced that £Nm of benefit. And that is the challenge actually to look at those sort of initiatives (HR director).

The uncertain financial case

The difficulty of making the investment case also emerged in answer to the question, 'What stops you investing more in your human resources?' Fifteen interviewees answered this question by talking about the difficulty of knowing what to do or where to spend money, or about the ambiguous link between such investments and performance outcomes. For example:

Umm, I think that it is probably the fact that it is extremely hard to prove that what you have invested, on its own, makes a difference. I mean, we are investing infinitely more in our people than we were three years ago, but I don't think we are investing enough in the people. Umm, and so I think there is a constant battle to demonstrate that you are getting a reward for what you are doing and this is a much more flaky, imprecise area, than if you publish a book...you can do an analysis and you can see how much it costs...it is very neat. These things are not like that...It is rather like what Lord Lever, or whatever his name is, said about advertising, he knew half of it worked but he didn't know which half! And that is absolutely the case with these programmes (operational director).

It's a bit like a marketing budget, you know, people always say, half of what I spent is ineffective but I don't know which half it is and I think it is a bit like that with people...What stops us spending more, I would say two things. One is quantifying the benefits, so you know identifying those things that are really going to make a difference to building business, and the second thing is just overall affordability in the financial envelope that we operate in (operational director).

Probably two things. One is the budget. Budget constraints. And two, lack of any scientific knowledge of how much is enough. So, do I think that, you imagine a scale of one to 10…On a scale of 1 to 10, do I think doing nothing is the right answer to the question in terms of people maintenance for want of a better term? I am absolutely convinced that is wrong. But do I know how much I have to spend to maximise value before I get into diminishing returns or anything else? I haven't got a clue (operational director).

Initial conclusion

In total, 29 of the 48 interviewees (60 per cent) made some comment about the difficulty of knowing how to implement progressive HR practices, how to quantify the benefit of doing them, or knowing where to invest money and how much to invest. Seven were CEOs, nine were HR directors, and 13 were operational directors. This suggests that the uncertainties surrounding the *how* of implementation as well as lack of ability to make a convincing case for investment are an important part of the explanation for the lack of greater investment in progressive people management. Operational directors were particularly uncertain, with 13 of the 16 making some kind of comment in this regard.

Even those who claimed to be implementing progressive HRM commented on the difficulty of knowing how to keep getting better at doing it. For example:

I believe [the argument on Figure 15] but interestingly for companies like ours, I'm not sure it is discriminating enough. I think our challenges are the hows along these things. Because just

looking at it, I wasn't being glib, we do, I can show you examples of what we do against all of these and we probably think we do it pretty well. So I think to me this is partly value driven as well which is what you take time to do. Our problem is, I think, understanding how to keep getting better at some of these things, I think that is the important thing (CEO).

7 | Do executives believe they are already implementing progressive people management practices?

◪ **Most executives believe their companies are already implementing specific progressive HR practices.**

◪ **A significant number of executives believe line managers are more responsible than HR managers for realising the benefits of better people management practice.**

A fifth possible explanation for the limited uptake of progressive HR practices in the UK is that executives believe they are already implementing them, and therefore have nothing more that they need to do. We therefore asked our interviewees about the extent to which the progressive people management practices shown in Figure 15 were implemented in their organisations. We tried to find out which practices they thought they had implemented, and which they thought could be improved.

Extent of implementation of progressive HR practices

Figure 19 shows a count of all comments made that referred to each of these practices. The chart shows the distribution of comments about whether practices were implemented or not. The fact that a practice was not mentioned by an interviewee does not necessarily mean that it is not implemented in the organisation concerned. Interviewees were free to comment on each one or not, as they saw fit, and some made more than one comment about a single HR practice.

The most commonly implemented practice was *training*. Twenty-one interviewees commented that they invested considerable sums in training. Four

interviewees said that their training and development for managerial or professional employees was more extensive than for other staff, and one CEO said the opposite: that his organisation did not invest in training above shop-floor level and that management tiers were expected to engage in self-development. Fifteen interviewees made some comment about the difficulty of getting training right. For example, three said that although a significant sum of money is spent by their organisation, it could be more effectively targeted:

I think we spend a lot of dead money on training rather than necessarily determining exactly what training who needs. So if someone wants to go on this course, well, okay then, [they] may be interested. Rather than, you need to go on this course because there is a deficiency here…we are trying to fill a hole (operational director).

Our investment in training is actually when you add it up, pretty impressive, but it is a bit scatter-gun – it is not terribly focused and it is not linked to analysis of skills and capabilities gaps which is informed by the business planning/corporate planning process too much…Nobody says, well here is your PDP, we've actually worked out the skills gap in terms of what we know we need to

46 | **Voices from the Boardroom**

Do executives believe they are already implementing progressive people management practices?

> **'The most commonly implemented practice was *training*.**
> **Twenty-one interviewees commented that they invested**
> **considerable sums in training.'**

deliver next year to meet this particular corporate goal. There isn't that sort of analysis so that is where we have got a lot of work to do. But that is not to say that we don't still do a lot of training (CEO).

After training, the next most commonly discussed practice was *performance management*. Seventeen interviewees said their organisations did this. Two interviewees said that performance management was conducted only for certain groups of staff. Others said that its effectiveness varied according to the quality of the manager or that although systems were in place, the reality was that performance management, and more specifically performance appraisal, was not really happening:

Appraisal is going on in most directorates yes. And it varies because – and this is the issue about having your middle managers properly trained – it varies according to the calibre of the individual ward sister at the end of the day, or the middle grade nurse manager who has just been reorganised, yet again (operational director).

For example, we have [an] appraisal system, we have some sort of kind of anecdotal benchmarking that about 50 per cent of our staff actually have an appraisal. I'm not sure how – on a real objective basis that's a bit harder. When you go round and talk to people they have either had no appraisal at all or a really poor experience of it. So in terms of like the most basic mechanism for actually setting out expectations and objectives and actually monitoring someone against that, it just isn't happening (HR director).

Figure 19 | Distribution of executives' comments about whether specific HR practices are implemented in their organisations

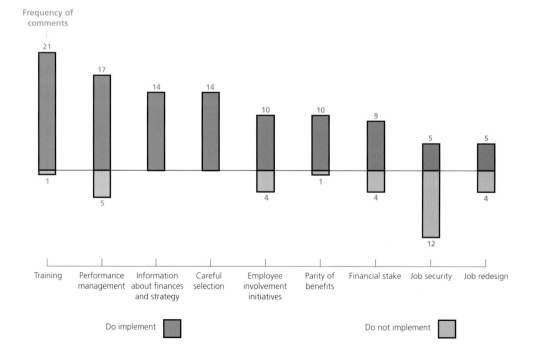

Fourteen interviewees said that they give employees *information about finances or strategy*. No executive said that this was something the organisation did not do, although one from the NHS pointed out how difficult it was to do in practice in a 24-hour service. Opinions were divided over whether it is possible to overdo communication. Fourteen interviewees said that their organisation did invest in careful *selection* to hire consistently with job requirements and organisational culture. No interviewee admitted to not being careful about selection, although five acknowledged that it is all too easy to get selection wrong:

Careful selection of hiring skills and abilities – well, I think we take the selection process very thoroughly although it seems to me that you can be as thorough and as careful as you like and still make the most howling mistakes. But I suppose if you didn't try then you'd make more mistakes (operational director).

Ten interviewees said they involved employees in *initiatives to improve workplace productivity*. Two (from the same organisation) mentioned Six Sigma initiatives. Two others from a manufacturing organisation mentioned initiatives to improve operational efficiency. Three mentioned business improvement or employee suggestion schemes. Four said this was not something they did. Ten comments were made about implementation of *equal benefits* and fair treatment throughout the organisation. Two of these were from the health service, where, as one CEO pointed out, there is a strong ethos around equal opportunities. Nine interviewees said that they did give employees a *financial stake* in the business, and four said that they did not, or that it did not apply to them. One executive from the NHS said that while she believed that it could help to motivate people, it

was not appropriate for her organisation since they could at best 'only play at it'.

Five respondents said that they did try to provide *job security*, or that they had managed to do so to a greater extent than competitors. One CEO said that he was convinced that the provision of job security was the source of his organisation's success:

I am absolutely convinced that one of the reasons that [this organisation] is relatively successful is continuity of employment and that is partly because you don't have this huge cost of transition and retraining, but also because we are basically not a product company, we are a service company, but it is relationship management particularly because a lot of our copyrights we don't have. The key skill we have is actually going out, is a kind of consulting skill…Our [suppliers] don't move around that much. They don't like to be dealing with people in production terms or marketing terms who then go, because they think, oh I have to re-educate this person, a waste of my time. So I am very aware, particularly in our industry, that staff stability, and stability of people full stop, is absolutely critical (CEO).

Two respondents from the NHS commented that job security was fairly irrelevant when they were desperate for people. Nine interviewees said that guaranteeing job security was not something that their organisations did or indeed could do:

There is no doubt that job security is important to people. When I was asked in the 80s in another organisation which I was then a part of, please just guarantee us employment, I said, I cannot do that and frankly, don't believe anybody who does. I said, but look around you, is the company investing in bricks and mortar and machinery and

> **'...progressive or high-commitment HR practices...important for higher organisational performance are by no means universally implemented in the organisations we visited.'**

training? Is it investing, if it is a branded goods manufacturer, in the marketplace? Can you see from information provided whether the company is increasing its market share, holding its own or falling back? These are the things that you should look to give you the comfort level that there is job security for you. But do not believe any manager that stands up before you and says, I guarantee your job security. That is not a real world and I have never said that, and never will (CEO).

A number of interviewees were baffled by what *job design* or *job redesign* meant, and confused it with involving employees in initiatives to improve workplace productivity. Five interviewees said their organisations were doing some kind of job redesign, although they tended to talk about maximising employees' performance in their roles, rather than changing the job to allow them greater responsibility and autonomy. One CEO did comment on the difficulty of designing jobs to maximise potential:

I would say that in order to maximise potential of anybody, the most important thing is their desire to do so. I don't think it is something that quite honestly redesigning their job or doing something centrally is going to give them...I mean certain people want to have eight hours for work, eight hours for rest and relaxation and eight hours in bed. And it wouldn't matter what you made their job, however interesting it was, that is the way they want to live (CEO).

This section has shown that progressive or high-commitment HR practices of the sort identified in the model in Figure 15 as important for higher organisational performance are by no means universally implemented in the organisations we visited. While the questioning process does not allow us to be confident about the extent of

application, the range of comments challenging the desirability, extent or impact of specific practices indicates doubts among executives about how valuable they consider some of these practices to be.

Desired improvements to implementation of progressive people management practices

Another way to assess the extent of implementation of progressive HR practices is to see whether executives think they could or should improve upon their implementation. Three executives observed that they thought every area could be improved. Another eight interviewees made some reference to the implementation of progressive HR practices as being an aspiration, something that could always be improved, or a journey rather than a destination.

I think they are done but inevitably they can always be done better. There is nothing on that list I guess I would say is kind of below a 5 out of 10, but there is nothing I would particularly say is a 9 out of 10 either. So yeah, I think all the ground is covered but the trick is in continuing to be really really effective in what we do (HR director).

I think this kind of [appraisal] form has helped us translate the conceptual six values into something that is constructive feedback for the 100 senior leaders. And that is, I think, allowing us to make more progress, get more traction on the improvement of living out the aspiration (CEO).

As far as individual HR practices are concerned, Figure 20 shows the distribution of comments about whether the implementation of these practices could be improved. Of the practices listed in Figure 15, *performance management* was the area where the largest number of respondents identified that improvements could be made. Nineteen respondents gave some kind of indication that they would like to improve it. For example:

Performance appraisal, feedback and personal development based on that process would be the single most important step forward, I think, that we have to take in HR management over the next couple of years…It is not sufficient – it is necessary, it is not a sufficient condition – to deal with the problems I have alluded to, but it is a very important plank that will make people feel that they have got a stake in the place and its success if they are getting some feedback in a systematic way (CEO).

I think that measuring individual performance is hugely important and I don't think we are doing that well enough. We have a system in place but that has got to be driven much much more robustly this year by the group managing directors because it is going to be so critical for them in achieving the succession planning. If they don't do that then they are not developing their people,

they are not identifying the training needs, consequently they are not preparing people to go into the slots that are available (HR director).

A number of the comments above, and other comments relating to performance management, were about improving the way managers deal with the performance of their team members. There was a good range of other comments about the need to improve the way managers manage, including the need to communicate better, and the need to take greater responsibility for HR issues and management. These comments are represented by the bar on Figure 20 labelled *line management*.

Five of these comments were from respondents in professional services organisations, and seven from the public sector, where executives wanted to inject managerial thinking into managers and team leaders. For example:

I actually think the staff have had a pretty poor experience of being managed in this organisation…We have to do quite a lot of work

Figure 20 | Distribution of executives' comments about desired improvements to progressive HR practices and other aspects of people management

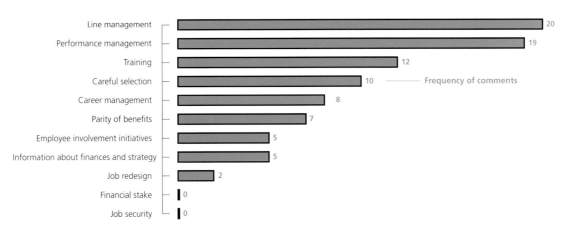

to make sure that [that changes]. I think what we are trying to do is infuse basic HR competences into the organisation at line manager level (operational director).

The culture we are trying to achieve here is one where managers see themselves as people who enable their staff to achieve their job description, their objectives or the business plan, to their greatest ability. That is where I want people to be and I will have them recite it like a mantra as well as underpinning it with systems and with reward systems and with IPR systems, all of those things. That is the culture we are trying to achieve, and I want it repeated like a mantra at trust board level...So it is actually about putting in all of the foundations that start to make that complete change of managerial focus (HR director).

An absolutely key group in the hospital is the ward manager, ward sister, that is a critical role, key leadership role – that's a very significant group of staff, front line of service. As we try to introduce change and try to get that group to take responsibility for things, they have found it hugely difficult to accept that responsibility for their staff as they see it conflicting with their patient responsibility (HR director).

These comments are interesting because they illustrate a perception that the drive for high-performing employees is something that should infuse the whole organisation, not just be implemented through a number of policies and practices. The idea that line managers, rather than HR professionals or HR practices, are responsible for realising high performance was mentioned by as many as 17 interviewees. For example:

This heading [HR Practices eliciting high performance – in Figure 15] irritates me. I don't think it is HR practices, I think it is the way the

businesses work with their people. HR sounds like imposed processes on a business and we are trying to move away from that. I think it is just the way we manage our people produces these things...I think the business should really only own the issues, have the responsibility and the HR professionals should support them and I think in some areas of our business it has gone the other way where it seems that the business no longer feels it has responsibility because it's HR that is doing it (HR director).

I think that the human resource function, it is a bit like marketing, the human resource function has a job to perform when it comes to payroll, compensation, all that stuff, the admin stuff, and therefore it has a duty to run that as cost effectively and efficiently as it can and be as up to date with the modern practices as it can given its environment. So that is the sort of machine bit that it does, that is the factory bit. But the piece on top of that is the most important piece. And that is true of any business. In marketing I have a responsibility to do certain things, like a factory. On top of that, how I get them to act with flair, creativity, make the right connections, share best practice, manage their projects properly and then stay for two years and then go and get another good job within the organisation – that is human resource management really and I consider that to be the most important part of my job (operational director).

Good managers will find their way through all that mumbo jumbo in two seconds flat. Bad guys you can lead them to the water, flog them, kick them, do anything you like to have better HR practices and they won't do it (CEO).

Ten interviewees said that *selection* was an area that they could improve. Five of these were in public sector organisations; three respondents

> **'It may...be that the difficulty of guaranteeing job security is not necessarily seen as incompatible with attempting to manage careers, in contrast to the suggestions made by some recent commentators.'**

from NHS organisations talked about tight labour market conditions (particularly for nurses), and the need to maintain quality in selection despite a desperate need for labour. Three HR directors from commercial organisations referred to the war for talent, and argued that they needed to be more creative about who they target and how they profile the organisation as an employer.

Twelve interviewees said that *training* was an area that they would like to improve. In some cases, this related back to earlier comments about whether it was being effectively targeted. Eight interviewees also talked about the wider area of *career management* and succession planning as something they could do better. For example:

Are there others that would elicit high performance? Umm. Well one of the things in our organisation that does, I am convinced, help retention and elicit high performance is moving people around the organisation, be it in territory or around the world...And there is a very clear link around secondments and deployment of people in our organisation and retention and we can clearly show that the percentage of people that go overseas come back and will stay (CEO).

One thing that we don't do much at all, and makes us very vulnerable is that there is no real succession planning...We don't do, what we should do, much more of this: say that we'll take you out of your job group, whilst you are a wizard at what you are doing, if you want to be a chief executive you've got to go and do something else. No good you saying, well I'll apply for that job – most other people will be much more able to do it than you. There are some cultural barriers, not very strong ones but there are some cultural barriers about doing that at the moment. I think that will make a great deal of difference. Show that the health service does develop people and

their careers and does not just leave it to happenstance (HR director).

In the context of the many recent accounts about the demise of the career and the job for life, the expected utility of career management as a means to develop future leadership is interesting. It also provides a contrast to the generally pessimistic sentiment expressed about being able to provide job security (see above). It may be that the comments about career management related to managerial or professional groups of employees, while comments about job security related to other groups. It may also be that the difficulty of guaranteeing job security is not necessarily seen as incompatible with attempting to manage careers, in contrast to the suggestions made by some recent commentators.[1]

Seven interviewees said the provision of *equal and fair treatment and parity of benefits* was an area they would like to improve upon. Only one of these improvements related to reducing hierarchical levels and status privileges within the organisation. Other comments related to gender equality (mentioned by three interviewees) and to ethnic minority staff. Ethnic minority initiatives were mentioned by respondents from the health service and by two from a manufacturing organisation, which hoped to improve its ethnic representation at management levels to reflect the make-up of its production workforce and its customer base.

Five respondents said that giving staff *information about finances and strategy* was an area they thought they could improve upon. Five said they thought they should do more to involve employees in *initiatives to improve workplace productivity*. Two respondents, both from the health service, said that *job redesign* was something they would like to do more of, while one operational director thought that this was 'a bit aspirational' for the health service.

Initial conclusion

Here we have seen that executives do believe they are already implementing some of the HR practices that are thought to be associated with superior business performance. The implementation of specific practices was mentioned 107 times. However, almost as many (94 comments) conveyed a desire either to introduce or improve upon particular practices. This suggests that executives do not think they have reached a point where high-performance HR practices, either individually or collectively, are fully implemented in their organisations.

That said, the most frequently cited focus for improvement related not to a specific HR practice but to the more general issue concerning the quality of line management. Of the 48 interviewees, 28 (58 per cent) spoke of the need to make managers more effective at leading, motivating and managing the performance of their staff. Thus, it seems that one major issue relating to the implementation of HR practices concerns the fabric of human interaction within the organisation. Line managers need to internalise the importance of people management for it to be effectively implemented. The analysis here suggests that the role and perceptions of line management may be a key factor militating against the implementation of progressive HR practices.

This section has focused on the implementation of individual HR practices. Proponents of the benefits of HR practices argue, however, that such practices need to be implemented in a coherent high-performance work *system*, where employees operate in a high-trust, high-involvement environment. We did not explicitly ask our interviewees about whether they had a high-performance work system in place. However, it is interesting that job redesign, employee involvement and even training were given relatively low priority as areas for improvement. These practices are often considered to be among the most fundamental to high-performance work systems. Whilst there was acknowledgement of room for improvement, and indeed the aspiration to improve, for the majority of interviewees that improvement appears to be based on making certain practices (selection, training, performance management) more effective, rather than effecting a full-scale step change towards a high-performance work system.

In summary, most executives believe that their organisations are already doing quite a lot to implement specific HR practices but at the same time acknowledge that there is scope to do more. In articulating this, many executives imply that there could be improvements in implementation of practices or that they could be applied more professionally. The focus was not always on the introduction or improvement of a practice because of its likely effect on business performance. In distinguishing scope for improvement from a belief in the business benefits of improvement in application of practices, there was some implication that better people management would be 'nice' rather than 'necessary'. This raises the question of whether there is any great urgency to improve people management and indeed whether this is an organisational priority. The next section addresses this issue.

Endnote

1 See for example, 'Career evolution'. *Economist*. 29 January 2000.

8 | Do executives embrace progressive people management practices as a priority?

☑ **Most executives endorse the view 'people are our greatest asset', but dislike the cliché.**

☑ **Half of interviewees thought other aspects of the business take precedence over investment in people.**

Another possible reason for the limited uptake of progressive HR practices in the UK is that senior managers do not view them as a priority. To explore this question, we turn to two distinct sets of answers to our interview questions. We wanted to know whether employees, as a collective group, were considered to be important to the organisation's success, and whether, in consequence, progressive HR practices were seen as a means to make the most of them. We therefore asked our interviewees whether their employees were 'their most important asset'. We hoped that the use of this familiar cliché might provoke comments about the relative importance of other resources. We also tried to find out whether progressive HRM was embraced as a priority by asking about factors that constrain investment in it. Where answers referred to the demands of other stakeholders as taking precedence, we felt we could conclude that progressive people management practices were not embraced as a priority, at least not as a top priority.

Are employees perceived to be the organisation's most important asset?

By asking our interviewees, 'Are your people your most important asset?' we hoped to explore executives' perceptions about the relative importance of their people versus other resources or business assets. To elicit this information in the interview setting, we first made the observation

that, 'Some CEOs like to say that their people are their most important asset.' Then, we asked CEOs whether they subscribed to this view. HR and other directors were asked whether their CEO subscribed to that view, and whether it was subscribed to generally in their organisation.

As we expected, many contradictory views emerged. The majority of respondents agreed with the sentiment that 'people are our more important asset', but many took issue with the terminology. The phrase was also roundly dismissed as hypocritical, meaningless, trite, or too easy to say but hard to put into practice. Several interviewees said they preferred other ways of saying how important employees are, or wished they knew how to express the sentiment differently. And, importantly, there was a set of responses that were concerned with the need not only to *say* that employees are important, but to *treat* them accordingly. Here we will concentrate on the positive and negative responses, and perceived deficits in how employees are treated.

People are our most important asset

There was a clear sentiment amongst the interview sample that employees are an extremely valuable and important resource. Of the 48 respondents, 37 made some kind of positive agreement that people were their most important asset. Employees were referred to as the organisation's only asset, as generators and drivers of business, as the source

> 'The majority of respondents agreed with the sentiment that "people are our more important asset", but many took issue with the terminology.'

of competitive advantage, as the organisation's only product or trading base, and as facilitators to make other assets productive. For example:

I think everyone would agree at a conceptual level that people are the most important asset. I think even [in] an old technology industry, I think we did studies that showed, perhaps five to seven years ago, that our intangible assets, our knowledge, was worth more than our physical assets and that the tide had really begun to change even for us (CEO).

If I think back to your original question – are employees important – yes. They are so important in the nature of the business that we do, the vast majority of our business is transacted by our people or with other people within our client firms, we've seen the way that we employ new people they bring business with them, when people leave business goes with them (CEO).

People are not our most important asset

Seven respondents were prepared to argue that their employees were not their most important resource. One CEO commented:

In reality our single most important asset are our clients because…they are the whole basis on which we can make any money at all (CEO).

Three interviewees argued that a thriving business is more enduring than any single group of people. People can always be attracted to join, or replaced if they leave. One CEO claimed that his company's brand and infrastructure were more important than its employees:

You know, the honest truth is, for me the reductio ad absurdum to that statement, is if all my people

left and there was just me, I have a fantastic brand, I have fantastic technology and to be honest the people of Great Britain would still get served [brand name] and so really if you are hard-nosed about it, the brand is actually my biggest asset. Now I don't think I can grow at the rate I would want to grow with that kind of mindset but if you were to step back and say, well is it your biggest asset – actually not because we have a success model which is not people dependent to run in extremis – we could always hire people to run it, I think where the challenge is – is how do you grow. So, it sounds like hypocrisy with all these big chief execs saying – people are my biggest asset. I am not sure they are (CEO).

But are people treated as the most important assets?

There was a commonly held view that, if you say your employees are your most important asset, you should treat them accordingly. Twenty-five interviewees made some reference to this. For example:

Very often you commoditise the people, because it is actually quite difficult if you say your people are your most important asset then you've got to then invest in the same kind of management processes of your people and their value as you would anything else. You know, you think of the tremendous amount of effort that businesses put in to look after their technology, their machinery, their money, and then you look at how much they invest to look after their people, it doesn't add up. So there is a sort of, don't tell me the words, show me how much you are actually spending on your people, and okay, you've got the wage bill, but just looking at how much are you spending to make sure they've got their right environment in total, what do they need as the environment in

Voices from the Boardroom | **55**

Do executives embrace progressive people management practices as a priority?

order to perform as opposed to the environment you give them, and are you prepared to just treat that cost as an extension of all the other business costs? So that the people can actually optimise the whole sum, because it is an optimisation of the whole (operational director).

Although almost half of the interviewees talked about the need to treat employees as if they were the organisation's most important asset, few offered suggestions about how this should be done. Perhaps tellingly, only three respondents referred to HR practices as a means to do so; and none were HR directors. In the first excerpt here, the speaker refers to the list of HR practices that was in front of him at the time:

I think people say those words but seldom believe it. And I think the way you make it happen is not by those statements but by the actions you take. And it is the actions you take which will indicate I think whether genuinely people are, or people are not. And to me, it then does come down to the things which are on this [Figure 15] (operational director).

I mean, if you believe your people are one of your most important assets which is definitely the case here, then you need to do everything possible to do all these things to motivate, train and all the rest of it. Now, some of those things involve the day-to-day influence of lawyers, some are wider HR things which just need proper structures and should be done by professionals and therefore I think they are integral (operational director).

Moreover, many of the interviewees who talked about the need to treat employees as the most important asset also said that this was not done in their organisation. Seventeen of them made comments to imply that there was some kind of

deficit in the way employees were treated. The first interviewee quoted below observed that his CEO would agree that people were his most important asset, while the operational leaders of the business would take a more instrumental attitude:

Yes. He would [agree the people are his most important asset]. Without doubt. I think [CEO, Chairman] and I would all say they are. Some of the operational leaders might not. Some operational leaders might say, bring them in, pile them high, flog them for what you get them for, and pump them out (operational director).

Whether we have always treated them [our people] as [our greatest asset] is a different matter and, probably there is a growing realisation that certainly here, we need to think about how we treat people differently because the world is just very different now (operational director).

Factors taking priority over investment in progressive HR practices

In response to the question, 'What stops you investing more in your human resources?' a set of answers emerged that implied that other stakeholders took priority. Fifteen references were made to other stakeholders, such as shareholders, customers, clients or regulators, taking precedence over employees. Five of these responses came from the public sector, as the following examples demonstrate:

We are umpteen million pounds in the red this year, we are going to have to cut patient services, you know, we are not going to spend money on this. No way (operational director).

We are running a £5 million deficit at the moment and we have to meet waiting list targets, trolley wait targets and we have to comply with controls assurance and clinical governance regimes in everything we do. So if we are going to move money into these areas we have to find £5 million to get back to break even and still be sufficient and find efficiency savings by doing things as yet we haven't identified and that enables us to meet all of those targets and keep to all of those standards (CEO).

Customer demands were also salient for five interviewees in the private sector:

At the end of the day, the only way we are going to maintain the business is by satisfying the customer, so that is the focal point for everybody, it is the customer that pays the wages and I think employees recognise that. So it is not management rhetoric around why we have to do certain things, we are trying to respond to the customer (HR director).

The remaining interviewees mentioned analysts' or market expectations. For example:

Umm, probably the dreaded [staff] cost income ratio. We have got it down from 70 per cent to 52 per cent but the analysts are still obsessed with it. It forces organisations of our size to be more concerned with head count than with costs because the analysts seize upon it and it becomes, because it can be translated into newsworthy items, so…for any financial organisation, keeping costs under control has a market significance (HR director).

Initial conclusion

Most executives endorse the sentiment that 'our people are our most important asset'. They do so reluctantly, partly out of dislike of an overused and rather empty cliché and partly because they acknowledge that while it may be true, their organisation does not treat people as if they are their most important asset. Indeed, of the 48 interviewees, 24 (50 per cent) made some kind of comment indicating either a deficit in the way people in the organisation are treated, or suggesting that other aspects of the business take priority over investment in human resources. Although many interviewees referred to the need to treat employees as if they were the organisation's most important resource, only three referred to human resource practices as a means to do this.

These data suggest that at least half the executives thought that progressive people management is not embraced as a priority for their organisations. In some cases financial deficits and difficult business conditions were cited as higher priorities; sometimes other stakeholders received greater priority. However, leaving aside the priority attached to people management, there may be other factors that constrain their adoption and implementation. The following chapter considers some of these other factors.

9 | Is the implementation of progressive people management practices constrained by other factors?

◘ **CEOs emphasise cultural constraints preventing the implementation of more progressive HR practices.**

◘ **Other managers emphasise financial or business constraints such as the drive for short-term profit.**

We asked our interviewees what stopped them investing more in their human resources. Some of the answers have already been covered, notably the difficulty of knowing how to do it or how to assess the outcomes, and the need to respond to the demands of other stakeholders. Four other constraints also emerged: factors relating to people in the organisation, financial constraints, cultural constraints and the day-to-day pressure of business.

People constraints on the implementation of people management

The first set of responses referred to constraints imposed on the implementation of progressive HR practices by *people* or groups within the organisation. These comments related to people's failure to acknowledge the importance of managing people or their lack of the necessary skills to do so. Eight of these comments concerned senior management's or board members' opposition. For example:

You know, the first survey in 1996 there was a dreadful struggle over it. Appraisal in the early 90s, I nearly got fired for trying to get appraisal going; there was a revolt in the partners' dining room (HR director).

We've got two groups on the board, the integrators such as myself and the resource managers, the people that run the business and they are tasked to deliver profit and we are tasked to deliver sustainable long-term performance. And there is tension between the two groups and because those people actually own the resources. In a time when profit is, shall we say is not going up at the rate one might possibly desire it to go up at, they are squeezing the pips and they are pushing, always pushing towards this concept of the efficient frontier, of operational efficiency, rather than standing back and saying, well let's fundamentally redesign the system. And so the tension is: I am into 'let's fundamentally redesign the system' and they are saying, 'we haven't got time, we haven't got time, got to keep squeezing the pips' (operational director).

Twelve comments related to middle management, or line management more generally. Executives talked about managers' lack of skills or capability, their reluctance to take responsibility for managing staff, and unwillingness to spend time talking with their staff. For example:

Beyond [money], I think it is a question of culture that we have discussed, and management capability. Particularly with some of these new managers, these clinical managers, they won't have the skills initially, they won't have developed the skills over time as you would expect in managers who have been around a long time, umm, to understand the significance and importance of this and then how to implement this (CEO).

And frankly some people manage in a very sort of blinkered way about managing the outputs and forgetting actually that you've got people around you who want to be managed in a different way so the input has to be organised and enabled as it were, so it is a big – I don't deny it is a major change, and some of the biggest problems are the middle management who have got to where they are because of coming through a certain path (HR director).

You can sometimes get resistance from managers who don't want to change the way they do things or who have a very autocratic style and don't want to spend time talking to their staff about the decisions or justifying the decisions or this kind of thing. So when I think about the blocks we've got in HR, none of them are money: time is one, winning over individual managers is one, and I suppose just getting things changed (HR director).

A further six comments about constraints on the implementation of high-performance work practices related to the quality or ability of people in the HR function. The first speaker is referring to the constraints imposed by his own function:

Lack of resources in the HR function. Umm. These [high-performance work practices] are complicated things. Lack of resources. We are rather tight organisations, investment banks, we don't carry people. We don't have lots of people who we can take out and say, here's a project, do it. Everybody is earning their corn and the bright people in the

front office are there to deliver. So we have the brain power, we just don't have surplus capacity to actually think through what all of this means (HR director).

One of the main reasons, a simple and practical one really, is that in the time I have been here, of all the different facets of my department, the one I have been least satisfied with has been the personnel outfit here…and I actually think, I have had seven personnel officers, I've tried ever so hard, and you know how crucial those posts are, to get the right people in post, really struggled and it is a very stressful job here, very stressful (operational director).

I guess, coming back to your point [about what stops me investing more in my human resources], I didn't have confidence and don't really still have confidence in the HR function to leave the – I don't think they are thought leaders yet. I think we've got some bright people there but I don't think they are, there is still a slight distance between what I think an aligned HR function could be with [this company] and what we've got (CEO).

Financial constraints on the implementation of people management

Twenty-six comments were made about *financial constraints* on the implementation of progressive HR practices. Of the 12 interviewees from public sector organisations, 11 made reference to some aspect of financial constraint, such as running a deficit fighting to stay within budget, or difficulty in prioritising expenditure. For example:

Umm, well the obvious headline constraint is money, like every trust, every hospital, the amount of money we have is insufficient to do all the things that we want to do. But no matter how

Voices from the Boardroom | **59**

Is implementation of progressive people management practices constrained by other factors?

'**A large set of comments were made about *cultural factors* constraining the implementation of HR practices.**'

much money we are given, that will always be the case. If they double the amount of money that they gave to me there would still be aspirations, people aspirations that weren't being met (CEO).

Well it is sheer money. The members don't have a problem investing in our people and training budgets or in high-tech developments, but we have all got to prioritise that against direct service provision. How do you balance a new investment of £1 million in IT with whether somebody gets cared for at home or, you know, in one of our residential care homes or whether we put a new block on a school (CEO).

The remaining comments about financial constraints related to the exigencies of capital structure and pressure to deliver short-term profit:

You know there are some tough questions, you know, profit is important. If someone said would you trade off your training budget for your profit target, I'd say yeah, yes I probably would, you need to know that. If you do it every year, you shouldn't have me as an MD, but in extremis as a one-year thing, would I say can I elongate the training horizon – yeah, I would (CEO).

The financial position of the company is the smart answer you know, we are about 100 per cent geared at the moment, we are pushing our luck in so many ways. We owe about £1.9 billion. So if it is the choice between winning a project in China to produce £20 million of profit over the next five years, or spend a similar (it would probably cost you £0.5 million to bid for a project like that), or spend £0.5 million on leadership development, one would win out over two, because we need the money (HR director).

Short-termism: we run the business very, very short term. Not as short term as a US corporation with quarterly earnings, but we are always chasing short-term profit (operational director).

Four interviewees stated explicitly that they did not think money was the constraining factor; it was time demands or cultural factors. One CEO said that even if his organisation was not constrained financially, he would not invest more in human resources.

Cultural constraints on the implementation of people management

A large set of comments were made about *cultural factors* constraining the implementation of HR practices. These 25 comments related to institutionalised attitudes, poor communication, a lack of empowerment or resistance to change. For example:

There are many initiatives that were developed in respect of employees, some of which you can see have been very positive and there are other areas where you can see that it isn't quite what employees are ready for. For instance team-based work systems. We saw tremendous benefits in moving forward with team-based work systems in terms of empowering employees, making sure that decision-making was at the most appropriate level in the organisation, that people had greater control over their work, and that we felt would respond to the aspirations of employees and equally would clearly provide increased gain and productivity to the organisation. The reality of it is that not all employees want that (HR director).

60 | **Voices from the Boardroom**

Is implementation of progressive people management practices constrained by other factors?

Nine of these comments related to the difficulty of achieving change, or the long delay between putting in place new work practices and seeing a result in terms of improved business performance:

Sometimes it just takes a long, long time to deal with people. Quick-fix approaches to communication, convincing people of today's message, changing behaviour, don't in my view work, except when you are in crisis: blast the place open, close it down and start again. So a lot of these things are in place but they take time (operational director).

You can't come in and do a job like this for a year and, I don't think, make a significant difference. Perhaps come in and make yourself unpopular and shake people up a bit but you couldn't actually in a year achieve that much. Organisations clearly take time to move forward and these types of organisation take quite a long time to move forward (HR director).

Constraints imposed by competing day-to-day demands

Finally, the fourth set of comments related to the day-to-day *demands of doing business*. Seven references were made to time constraints.

I think it is pressure, the fact is they have deadlines to meet, they have products to deliver, within cost constraints and revenue requirements and all that kind of stuff, and so from time to time they get in the way, if you want (laughing), of how people would like to organise themselves (HR director).

I think where we've got areas where we want to see more, it isn't actually finances that is holding it back. There are a number of things, one of the biggest is time. Time is a much bigger problem

than money in our industry; that may not be true in other industries, but we are doing well as a company. We have lots of HR plans and initiatives that are supported by the board but it is time (HR director).

I don't think it is really money. It is that there are only so many hours in a day. How do you balance the needs of trying to run the business in terms of turning out products, supplying water, whatever, whilst investing the effort of trying to help people to grow and develop? (CEO).

A further seven comments were made about pressure, tasks, or the 'press of day-to-day urgent problems', as one CEO put it:

The pressure is on, on the service end, on visible social services, on front line staff. And I think there is an increased awareness now, an increasing awareness now – that in some ways the cutbacks on support staff have actually gone too far, have got beyond a point that it is possible to do anything other than just madly spin all the plates and try and keep them roughly up there (HR director).

Figure 21 shows a breakdown of the suggested factors constraining implementation of progressive HR practices by role. It shows that HR directors and operational directors were more inclined to cite people constraints. The HR directors talked about line managers not wanting to take responsibility for staff, and about a lack of commitment from senior management. The operational directors referred to poor delegation, the wrong mindset, or not having the skills to manage effectively.

CEOs were more likely to emphasise more entrenched aspects of organisational culture. They referred to people not wanting to be challenged

> '...a wide range of factors were cited as constraints on the implementation of progressive HR practices, including the skills and attitudes of people in the organisation, financial constraints and profit motive...'

by change, a 'counter-cultural' element, the time taken to instil change, difficulties in integrating different cultures after a merger and a lack of empowerment. For example:

There is a very strong culture of disempowerment [here] that I think we've discovered. It is really quite odd how really quite well-educated professional people don't seem to feel they have the power to suggest changes and to make improvements at the coal face, and what I always say to them on their induction is that they need to be stroppy, certainly as new members of staff, they need to feel they can be stroppy with their supervisors or their first line managers and ask the question – Why the hell are you doing it this way? It is beginning to happen but it is quite difficult to unravel it because everything is connected with everything else (CEO).

I think people are quite willing to consider doing things differently, as long as it doesn't involve them, as long as they don't have to change what they do! (laughs) That's day-to-day management (CEO).

Initial conclusion

We have seen here that a wide range of factors were cited as constraints on the implementation of progressive HR practices, including the skills and

attitudes of people in the organisation, financial constraints and profit motive, competing day-to-day pressures and the more intractable issue of organisational culture.

The CEOs' emphasis on cultural constraints is interesting, given that several models of leadership suggest that chief executives have a key role to play in managing and changing organisation culture. Our CEOs' comments reflect a realistic, rather than pessimistic outlook, and a recognition that it takes time to achieve change, particularly where that change relates to line management behaviour, which they identify as a key factor in implementing progressive work practices. One operational director put it like this:

If we also drive another message down the organisation, which we are, which is all about leadership and team-building and coaching and mentoring and that kind of thing, that really does require a very big change in human behaviour. Because you are looking at a legacy, you hired people 25 years ago in a particular culture and environment and you have brought them up for 25 years and nurtured them in a particular environment. If you change the environment, some people are going to change willingly, other people are not going to change at all and some people are going to take quite a long time to make the move from A to B (operational director).

Figure 21 | Distribution of comments about factors constraining implementation of progressive HR practices, analysed by role of interviewee

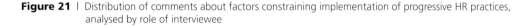

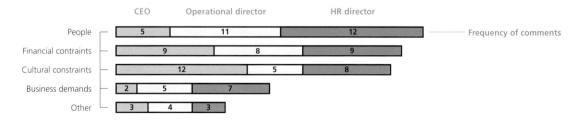

It is also interesting that people and cultural constraints together received slightly more comment than financial constraints and business demands (a total of 43 compared with 40). Critics of Anglo-Saxon models of management often argue that it is Britain's institutional short-termism that prevents the widespread adoption of high-skill, high-involvement workplaces. Our analysis suggests that the absence of a performance-driven, people-oriented culture amongst British managers may be as important a factor in explaining the limited uptake of progressive HR practices as short-termism or market pressures.

Voices from the Boardroom | **63**

Are executives sceptical about the role of HR departments and of HRM innovations?

10 | Are executives sceptical about the role of HR departments and of HRM innovations?

◘ **HR directors made the most negative comments about the role of the HR function.**

◘ **Executives believe HR managers need to have a good understanding of the business to make a positive contribution.**

◘ **Line managers are seen as likely deliverers of HR practices.**

A final possible explanation for the limited uptake of progressive HR practices in UK organisations is that executives are sceptical about the role and credibility of HR departments and of the innovations that might be associated with them. If the HR function, and the people within it, are seen as providing a specialist or purely administrative role, executives might think that human resource management has little relevance to the whole organisation. It is also possible that the behaviour of HR professionals causes their colleagues to be sceptical about human resource management. If their initiatives are seen as influence-seeking or as setting up new bureaucratic systems without benefiting the wider organisation, this may cause senior managers to see human resource management as of marginal importance.

We therefore asked our executives the following question: 'What role do you see for the HR function as a contributor to the firm's performance?' We collected a total of 45 answers to this direct question; 25 of these answers asserted a positive perception of the HR function as a contributor to business performance, while 20 were negative. Also emerging from the interviews were a further 163 comments about the HR function or the people within it. Some of these were negative or critical of the HR function, some were positive or supportive, and some were neutral.

Figure 22 shows the number of positive, negative and neutral comments about the HR function made by CEOs, operational directors and HR directors. It shows that HR directors made the most comments overall (92 comments out of 208), including the most negative and the fewest positive comments. This suggests that the HR directors participating in the research were far from satisfied with the performance of their own function. CEOs made the fewest comments overall, and their comments were more evenly matched between positive and negative, while operational directors were more inclined to be negative. The following paragraphs explore the substance of these comments in more detail. A total of 70 largely neutral comments were made about the role of the HR function. These are summarised in Figure 23. The positive and negative comments are summarised in Figure 24.

Relationship with the board and board-level executives

Nine interviewees made comments that related to HR's impact on board- or executive-level management. Two were CEOs; one of these (quoted below) said that he thought the HR director should be a member of the executive board, in order to send the right message to the organisation (although in fact this was not the case in his organisation). An operational director

'...HR directors participating in the research were far from satisfied with the performance of their own function.'

posed the opposite view: that the HR director should not be on the board because HR was everyone's responsibility:

By not having your HR director as a member of the board you are giving a message to people to say this isn't as important as some other things are (CEO).

We are just moving into an environment where we probably don't think there is a need for a separate HR person, completely separate HR person on the board. Because by having one you almost marginalise the responsibility for the whole board to deal with it (operational director).

The other six people who commented about board-level relationships were HR directors. One

HR director argued that most CEOs do not know enough about HR, and that HR directors should therefore seek to influence their CEO by 'managing upwards':

I think chief execs don't know enough about HR, I think very often chief execs have come through a particular part of the organisation where they perhaps don't always have the most pronounced HR skills themselves. We don't see many HR directors becoming chief execs. Within their natural peer group therefore those skills are perhaps not always as well developed as they need to be. So it is very important for an HR director to manage upwards. Particularly because up until recently the bottom line finance figures have been what interested them because that is what they were judged on and only latterly have they been

Figure 22 | Distribution of positive, negative and neutral comments about the HR function, analysed by role of interviewee

Figure 23 | Distribution of comments about the role of the HR function, analysed by role of interviewee

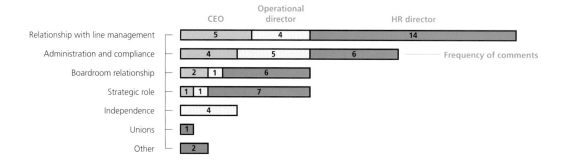

Voices from the Boardroom | **65**

Are executives sceptical about the role of HR departments and of HRM innovations?

judged, or will be judged, on HR performance if you like (HR director).

Two HR directors commented that HR directors are not widely represented at board level because the function has not proved itself sufficiently:

The HR people want to beat their way to the boardroom door, but what are they going to say when they get there? They don't understand the business (HR director).

You have to have the ear, you have to have the confidence to go in and tell people when it is awful, and tell them they've got to do something about it, so yes, it is about having the seat at the right table. And we read ad nauseum *about why aren't HR directors on the main board and my answer to that would be, because not enough of them have been able to prove the case that HR can contribute. It is there, it's there to be done (HR director).*

Fourteen positive comments were made (six from CEOs, five from HR directors, four from operational directors) about HR's relationship with board-level executives. For example:

Everything we consider has to be informed by the HR implications about how we are going to get our people to work in different ways or better ways, smarter ways. And so how we attract them in, how we keep them and actually how we let them go and how we develop them out of the organisation, how we manage that distinctive process consciously and strategically is at the heart of it and that is why the HR director is a full voting member of the board…We are a people organisation and as such it is unconscionable that we don't have the HR director on the board (CEO).

Five HR directors were positive about their influence at board level. In the first of these two quotes below, the speaker attributes his influence to a fair degree of discretion granted to him by the CEO. In the second, the HR director described his efforts to make the board recognise the importance of HR, and his use of research evidence to convince them. In four of the organisations represented by these five HR directors, positive comments were made about them by at least one of their colleagues:

The work going on [five years ago] was a major turning point, it really was a question of [the organisation] either had to get its act together or it was not going to survive, so, and that process opened up a recognition of the contribution of good HR practice, so there was an acceptance that things had to get better. So, that gave me an opening and a legitimacy as to justify my presence and my demands on the organisation, so that has been helpful. The previous chief executive I think had some very clear views about err, he wasn't a particularly strong HR person at all, some of his instincts were really quite crude and mistimed. (But) he did recognise there was a contribution for a professional HR (HR director).

I mean the attitude survey in 1996 was probably the most significant shift where even the senior partner at the time just sat on the fence. You know, he said, if you ask people it will create problems and so on. But [the current CEO] was great, he got behind it even though he had some worries about it and we basically forced it through. We just leant on people, got the right people on his side so they all said the right thing at the right time in the right meetings and it happened. And it was a shock to partners when they saw the results. One of the interesting things about it actually was

> **'The underlying supposition was that it is the line manager's role rather than HR's role, to "do" human resource management.'**

what one of the current board members said at the time, I never realised that you could use data to represent people issues. Because what we did was, do the survey, show how we stood up against various norms, but also I produced a lot of data relating to turnover statistics, trends, all sorts of things, which completely meshed in with this stuff, and they thought God, actually there is cause and effect here (HR director).

Three negative comments were made about the impact of the HR function at board level. One CEO said that he did not think his colleagues were 'thought leaders', while an operational director said that he didn't think HR played the sounding board role that was needed. Another operational director made a similar comment about a current HR director not being a 'thinking partner':

She is not my thinking partner the way [her predecessor] was on issues and how do we resolve organisation difficulties, right, but we want to get the training programme started and we want to get these X things fixed and we've got a huge issue with people on hack with payroll. Two weeks clear she's got it all done. There is a hugely different role between someone who is just absolutely good at getting things done and moving, and your thinking partner (operational director).

Relationship with line management

Twenty-three general comments were made about HR's relationship with line management. Twelve of these (four CEOs, six HR directors, two operational directors) asserted that the role of the HR function was to support line management. The underlying supposition was that it is the line manager's role rather than HR's role, to 'do' human resource management. For example:

I do fundamentally believe that the management of HR is a key task of the manager, it is not something that is done by HR professionals. The HR people are there to support managers in managing HR (CEO).

In addition to these 12 comments, five interviewees (two CEOs, two operational directors, one HR director) said they thought more responsibility should be passed on to line management, while the HR function became more of a 'service provider'. In contrast, one HR director argued that the line managers needed more assistance so that they could focus on the day-to-day jobs. Seven interviewees (two CEOs, four HR directors, one operational director) talked about the need for the HR function to be 'close to' and have a good understanding of the 'business'. For example:

What do I think buys credibility in this organisation particularly, you need to be able to talk the business language, so to your point, you need to have a results orientation so you need to be able to rather than just talk the business language, you need to be able to do the things which make you feel that you are part of its success, so you need to be able to show that you can respond and deliver the changes where they are needed (HR director).

Four positive comments were made about HR's relationship with line management. These suggested that, where HR professionals have come forward with ideas, they have been received positively by line managers. Eleven negative comments were made (four CEOs, two HR directors, five operational directors). The four CEOs were all critical of instances where HR had become too involved in matters that they saw as line management responsibility:

Voices from the Boardroom | **67**

Are executives sceptical about the role of HR departments and of HRM innovations?

Had a bit of that at [my former company] at one time too. When HR overstepped the mark of their importance and the generation of who was high potential and who wasn't, and who was on fast track and who wasn't, was HR's responsibility. It never should be. When that gets disconnected from what is reality, then you've got a load of ivory tower people trying to fill up positions in businesses that really matter, without the line management knowing and understanding what they've got, in terms of human material. When those two become disconnected, you've got chaos on your hands (CEO).

Several comments were to the effect that HR tends to constrain others' actions, by acting as the 'corporate policemen'. Others said that HR's isolation from the line had made it irrelevant, or misconstrued:

I am suggesting that the HR function needs to help the management move things on a lot quicker than it does at the moment. The HR function has a tendency to tell you the 15 reasons why you may not wish to do something. It doesn't have a tendency to say, but given your situation, if I was you, I would do this and this and wait and see what happens. That is what I think it should start doing. Because people get frightened of diversity issues and race issues and I am going to get sued, and this is going to happen and that is going to happen (operational director).

I suppose the thing that really gets up my nose about some of the way in which HR operates is: the worst thing we think you can do is make people feel they are units. If people feel they are a unit they will respond like a unit and no more, and that is the worst of all things, I think (operational director).

The strategic role of the HR function

Nine interviewees (including seven HR directors) mentioned the strategic role of the HR function. For all of these nine, the strategic role was more of an aspiration than a reality. One operational director said he thought HR's administrative role should be separated from its strategic one:

The payroll, HR queries, benefits, contract management, terms and conditions, and a helpline, and answering the phone and dealing with people, isn't just sitting on a computer screen punching numbers in, but that can be segregated from the policy and strategy piece – that is my personal view. So I don't think we serve ourselves best by leaving the two entangled with one another. Umm, and I think it would actually improve the strategy-setting and goal-setting of the really small smart bit, is really what the plc needs, the plc doesn't need to own the outsourced piece. But I think the most important thing for this company, for any company, any plc, is to figure out what needs to be set from the top and make sure that is done…I think a lot of companies struggle to figure out where the machinery ends and the policy and strategy begins. The more those can be disentangled I think gives clarity to vision of what should be created (operational director).

Four interviewees, all operational directors, made reference to HR's position as an *independent* function. Three of these asserted that it was valuable for HR to be independent, while a fourth argued, on the contrary, that it is impossible for the HR function to be independent:

And this notion of independence. That there is an independent function to talk to. It is a nonsense. You can't be anything independent in a business.

68 | **Voices from the Boardroom**

Are executives sceptical about the role of HR departments and of HRM innovations?

'Many commented that the perception that HR contributed to business performance depended on the calibre of the individuals in the HR function, or varied between parts of the business.'

A business is an interdependent entity. There is no part that you can say has 'independence' because all at the end of the day affects the business affects the bottom line. But it is nice to think that there is an independent body in a business (operational director).

The contribution of the HR function to business performance

Among the positive and negative comments, which are summarised in Figure 24, a number referred to the core issues addressed in this report, the contribution of the HR function and the people in it to the performance of the business

The distribution of positive comments about the HR function is shown in the upper half of Figure 24, and negative comments in the lower half. Twenty-five interviewees (six CEOs, six HR directors and 13 operational directors) said that they

thought the HR function made a positive contribution to the performance of the organisation:

I see them having a huge role in contributing to it – not the only role, but having a significant role in it, yes. In a way their role is to set the tone, set the policy and the strategy and if it is not delivering what needs to be done or they don't believe it is pointing in the right direction their job is also to provoke or confront issues and make sure that management is alert to what we are creating. So the role plays two ways – both downwards and upwards (operational director).

Only seven of these interviewees were wholly positive, however. The other respondents qualified their comments. Many commented that the perception that HR contributed to business performance depended on the calibre of the individuals in the HR function, or varied between parts of the business.

Figure 24 | Distribution of positive and negative comments about the role of the HR function, analysed by role of interviewee

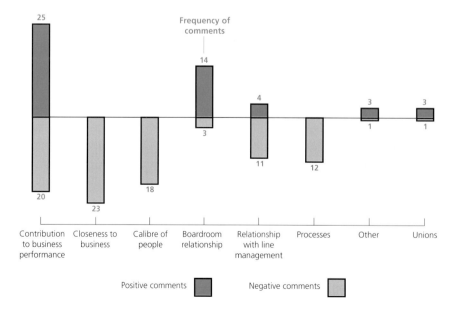

Voices from the Boardroom | **69**

Are executives sceptical about the role of HR departments and of HRM innovations?

Twenty negative comments were made about HR's contribution to business performance. Three were from CEOs, 11 from HR directors and six from operational directors. Several commented that HR is seen only as providing training, and that beyond 'the old personnel bit', as one HR director put it, their contribution is not really recognised. Others said that the contribution of HR was only recognised by senior management. These negative comments were as common from the HR directors as from others (although two of the HR directors who were most negative about their function attributed its low status to the behaviour of their predecessors). One CEO said that, while HR had previously made a valuable contribution, the function had now buried itself behind an edifice of bureaucracy:

We moved in the last two to three years to the worst of every world in my judgement, which is having a very large number of people who are all switched on and imaginative, they created a large number of processes to be followed and they have actually started to clog the organisation (CEO).

The closeness of the HR function to the business

Twenty-three negative comments (eight from CEOs, eight from HR directors, seven from operational directors) were made about the HR function's closeness to the business. Criticisms included that the career path was too narrow, that HR people were not experienced in management, and that the function was producing an output that the business did not really need:

When I went into it in the mid-70s the quality – well I would say that wouldn't I – for a variety of reasons it was higher than it is now. I think if anything the function has lost stature in that

period and not gained it. I think there is too much talk about strategic HR and business partnering and blah, blah, blah, blah, and too little actual work. Too much talk and not enough action (HR director).

So there is a very delicate and strong connection between the staff support that HR functions can give to an organisation and the fact that they can easily just get parted off and be in some sort of stratosphere where they are floating around, sucking in people from universities outside, processing them through multiplicities and training programmes and wonder why they can't get connected into the business or doing anything proper and they are always skidding around the outside, bumping up against the experience in the business, and never impressing anybody (CEO).

I think that is down to the quality of the people rather than the job they are supposed to be fulfilling. So, umm, the best HR people that I have ever worked with you can always have a sensible conversation with about the pressures in the business and the way the business is performing…I have worked with a number of HR professionals who I don't think are close enough to what is happening in the business and therefore aren't contributing in a general management sense as well as in a functional sense and a good HR person needs to do both (operational director).

Several of these comments related to the language that HR professionals tend to use:

I would like to think that the HR function is better regarded, much better regarded than it used to be. But there is a problem because the human resources professionals have I think talked themselves into a sort of area, or ghetto you know, where they are happier talking to each other sometimes, than they are actually being involved in the business…And I think one of the problems with the human resource function is that it has got sidetracked into a language that isn't actually ever the way people speak (operational director).

The ghettoism starts where there is not enough robust intellectual challenge. There is a huge problem with semantics in HR, which is what do all these words really mean that we continuously talk about and of all the functions in terms of its language and meaning – it is the most generalised set of language and words that any function in the business uses (HR director).

The calibre of HR specialists

Eighteen negative comments and no positive comments were made about the calibre of people in the HR function. Nine of these were from HR directors themselves, who made observations about the quality of the people the function attracts, and commented how difficult it was to hire people with the right skills:

So the overall quality of people in the HR function is a major problem – not just here I think, as I said, I am inclined to think that our people are quite good, they are quite good – but as a general statement the quality of people in HR is dreadful. And getting worse…To become a strategic business partner you need to have people who have backgrounds in consulting or possibly MBAs or something equivalent in the rest of the world, who are highly analytical, very effective communicators verbally and in writing and have outstandingly good interpersonal skills. Well, people who have that set of attributes would not find HR an attractive function to go into. It is a vicious circle (HR director).

Criticisms made of people in HR included that they lacked integrity, tended to overinflate their importance, or were of a low calibre. The following comments were some of the more outspoken:

I think HR are probably the worst practitioners of everything that we've been talking about. In my experience they are usually bloody awful. They are the worst at developing their people, they are the worst at managing their people, their people are usually the most dissatisfied in the organisation and they are usually the worst at doing what they primarily are there to do, which is the administration. So they are usually pretty poor. But they have grand ideas. And it is seen as a way to power (operational director).

One of the curious things about human resources functions is that they are often staffed by people who don't really like people very much. Some of the worst letters I have ever read to people about their conditions or so on, are written by people in the human resources function, who write letters and talk to people in a way that they would be aghast if anybody talked to them (operational director).

If there is one part of the organisation that doesn't look as if it takes HR principles that seriously, it is HR – now I don't know whether that is true in other organisations, but if you looked at some of the sloppy way HR recruits for HR, if you looked at the amount of training HR individuals go on themselves, if you look at how well the performance measurement systems work for HR executives, the answer is poor, poor and poor (operational director).

Voices from the Boardroom | **71**

Are executives sceptical about the role of HR departments and of HRM innovations?

> 'Fifteen interviewees...talked about the HR function's role as providing an administrative service...providing specialist services...or as providing technical advice on compliance issues.'

HR as an administrative bureaucracy

Fifteen interviewees (four CEOs, six HR directors and five operational directors) talked about the HR function's role as providing an administrative service (dealing with payroll, pensions etc), providing specialist services (such as assessment interventions) or as providing technical advice on compliance issues. Two operational directors said that the HR function should be reduced to administrative work, leaving the line responsible for 'human resource management'. A CEO argued that the HR function should shrink to a specialist role, and use agencies to deliver most of its services. In contrast, two HR directors wanted to outsource HR's administrative work and strengthen its role in providing a consultancy or advisory service to the rest of the organisation.

Twelve negative comments related to the processes and procedures that HR puts in place as being too onerous, bureaucratic or simplistic. Six of these were from HR directors:

There is a real risk that the HR industry creates material for use in an organisation, which my analogy is it clogs up the arteries of the organisation. Why do you need appraisal systems with lots of bits of paper, why do you need merit systems, why do you need a lot of the training that goes on? If we spent our money in a more focused way and focused around certain priorities, wouldn't the thing be more in perspective? (HR director).

But within our organisation we have an HR function which is steeped in process mindset to do with grading, competency frameworks, appraisal systems which have the design of a push me-pull you type animal which doesn't achieve anything. Glorious in their construct but bloody useless in their implementation (operational director).

Initial conclusion

In the paragraphs above we have explored executives' perceptions of the role and contribution of the HR function in some detail. We have seen that executives spoke most commonly about the function's relationship with line management, and that the majority of those who spoke about this thought that the primary responsibility for human resource management lies with line management, not the HR function. We have also seen that executives think it is important for HR professionals to have a good understanding of the wider business in order to assist their line colleagues in delivering their human resource management role, and that they are often perceived to have failed in that regard. One important reason for that appears to be related to the calibre of people in the HR function, which was widely regarded as poor, even by HR directors.

We have also seen that although HR directors in general appear to have a good relationship with board-level management, they are not expected to make a strategic contribution, even if this is something to which they aspire. Only five of the non-HR interviewees (three CEOs, two operational directors) talked about the need for an HR strategy, or for human resources to become aligned to business strategy. Thus it seems that opinions are mixed about whether the HR function does have a contribution to make to business performance, and that its contribution is primarily expected to be in a supportive, rather than a strategic or leadership role.

In the introduction to this report we postulated that one reason for the limited uptake of progressive HR practices in UK organisations is that executives are sceptical about the role of the HR function and of HR innovations. Here we have presented excerpts from our interviews to confirm that initiatives set up by the HR function are widely perceived to have little relevance to the wider organisation, or to be overly administrative or bureaucratic. Where these initiatives are seen as the main contribution of the HR function, then the influence of HR directors at board level and amongst other line managers is likely to be compromised by these perceptions. One issue on which the executives were largely silent was the role of fads and fashions. We had expected to hear rather more on this topic but in the relatively limited number of comments about HR innovations, the concern was much for the bureaucratic consequences than for their superficiality.

It is worth noting in passing that 10 of our interviewees were dismissive of the term 'human resource management', viewing it as signifying little other than a rebranding of the personnel function, or an attempt by personnel professionals to acquire for themselves a more strategic role. For these reasons, we might assume that many executives would be dismissive or sceptical of the argument that a more progressive approach to human resource management would benefit their organisation.

We also know, however, that human resource management is seen by many to be the responsibility of line managers, rather than of a specialised function (17 of the 48 interviewees said this explicitly). The following quote illustrates this well:

I draw a distinction between HR practice and an HR department. Because I think one of the failures – probably it is universal but it is maybe more true in the UK – is that every time we recognise a factor we set up a department to manage that factor whether it is quality or health and safety or

HR practice. We always say, oh you've got to give that facet of the business to a person, as if you can isolate that facet from everything else that you do. Whereas the reality is, it is holistic. Then the question is, how do you get that holistic understanding into the heads of the practitioners who've got to practice it, and in the case of HR the people who have got to practice it are the line people. There are some things that HR has to do but they are trivial compared to what the people on the ground have to do (operational director).

Where progressive human resource management can be presented not as a specialist innovation, or as a vague collection of practices but rather as a practical means to make line managers more effective in their management roles, it may have considerable appeal.

11 | Summary and conclusions

In this report we have presented the findings of a set of 48 interviews conducted with CEOs, HR directors and other board-level executives in 16 organisations. We have explored a number of suggested explanations for the apparently limited adoption of progressive people management practices in UK workplaces.

Are executives aware of the research findings that attempt to demonstrate links between people management and business performance?

About half of the executives we interviewed were not aware of the research evidence. Most of their ideas about people management come from experience or from internal sources, such as board-level colleagues and the wider organisation. There is a relative lack of openness to or interest in ideas from outside their organisation with reading material, consultants and management gurus rarely mentioned as sources of new ideas. This limited interest in external information will minimise the impact of research evidence on human resource management and corporate performance. Although, as might be expected, HR directors were more aware of this research, they do not appear to have communicated it effectively to senior colleagues in their organisations.

Are executives convinced by the research findings?

Most of our interviewees considered it self-evident that good people management affects organisational performance. They were mostly prepared to accept, in broad terms, the argument made by advocates of progressive people management, but in most cases this was because of what they already believed rather than because of any new model or research evidence. Also, a

degree of doubt and scepticism was expressed when presented with the evidence that has been collected in support of this argument. Our interviewees questioned whether the findings told the whole story, and were unsure whether they were of sufficient relevance to their organisations to justify any change in their current practices. As confident senior executives, they trusted their experience and their own values considerably more than any research findings, however convincing and however well presented.

Do executives think it makes sense to implement progressive people management practices?

Despite some scepticism about the research evidence, almost all of our interviewees agreed with the broad argument that if you treat people well, business performance should be enhanced. However, they took issue with this argument when it was applied to a number of the specific practices. They were more likely to endorse some relatively specific practices such as selection and performance appraisal than less clear-cut practices such as employee involvement and job redesign. They endorsed and tended to emphasise effective management of people but did not see this as synonymous with or necessarily associated with the application of progressive human resource practices.

Do executives know how to implement progressive people management practices?

We found that the majority of executives were uncertain about how best to implement progressive HR practices. There was some scepticism about the ability to demonstrate financial returns and about whether 'more' is necessarily 'better'. Those who claimed already to

> '...almost all of our interviewees agreed with the broad argument that if you treat people well, business performance should be enhanced.'

be implementing progressive HR practices were uncertain about how they could do so better. Clearer guidelines about how to implement practices, based on successful cases, would be widely welcomed.

Do executives believe they are already implementing progressive people management practices?

We suggested that executives do not think they have reached a point where progressive HR practices are fully implemented. That said, most were more interested in improving what they currently do than introducing new practices; and they were interested in specific practices rather than a coherent bundle of activities. In so far as priority practices were identified, selection and performance appraisal were emphasised as key areas of current application where there was room for further improvement. Further investment in training, job design and provision of a financial stake were viewed with quite considerable scepticism

Do executives embrace progressive people management practices as a priority?

The majority of our interviewees did not indicate that pursuing a more complete or a more effective implementation of people management practices in their organisations was a top priority. In part this may be due to the fact that many of them see people management as part and parcel of line managers' day-to-day responsibilities, rather than as a separate initiative. Also many, while acknowledging they could do more, intimated that they feel they are already doing enough to get by.

Is the implementation of progressive people management practices constrained by other factors?

Four main kinds of constraint were identified. These were concerned with people, with financial resources, with the culture of the organisation and with competing day-to-day demands on time and resources. The most important issues concerned management of the organisational culture and the people within it, including in particular line management, who were seen to have a special responsibility for the delivery of effective people management, a responsibility they were sometimes not perceived to execute as they should.

Are executives sceptical of HR departments and HRM innovations?

The executives indicated some uncertainty about the appropriate role of the HR function and there was no consistent view of the part that it should play in people management. There was some desire to see it contributing to board-level activity and a recognition that this was sometimes achieved. On the other hand, a distinctive strategic contribution was seen as an aspiration rather than a reality. There was, once again, an emphasis on the responsibility of line managers to ensure the implementation of effective human resource management. The HR function was seen as sometimes making an effective contribution to business performance but specific initiatives, when they were mentioned, were often seen as too bureaucratic. In general, there was surprisingly little reference to specific initiatives or to fads and fashions. The HR directors were more critical of the

HR function than the other directors. On the basis of this evidence, the HR function is not seen as being in the vanguard of change irrespective of whether this is organisational change in general or more specific changes in human resource management.

Implications for the HR profession

The research presented in this report presents something of a paradox for the HR profession. On the one hand, the presence of a personnel specialist has been shown to be associated with significantly higher profit per employee (as we saw in the first part of this report). That may be because firms that employ personnel specialists tend to take people management issues more seriously. On the other hand, many of the senior managers interviewed, including HR directors, were critical of the contribution of the HR function, and of the calibre of the people within it.

According to our interviewees, the key players in making sure that good people management is achieved are line managers. Few HR managers would deny this. What is more difficult is the rather low value placed on the support they receive from the HR function.

That said, there is still much to play for in determining what the role of the HR function should be. Should it, for example, be proactive or supportive, centralised or contracted out? There was no clear consensus about how it should be organised. The most commonly held view was that HR should play a supporting role for line management. There was little expectation that beyond the HR director, the HR function could or should play a strategic role, or be active in shaping the 'people' component of business strategy.

However, since many senior executives rely on internal rather than external sources for their ideas, and to a very limited extent on reading material, HR directors are in a strong position to have an influence over their colleagues' ideas. They are generally perceived to have a positive relationship at board level. They need to make the most of this role. Their message should not be so much that good people management can have an influence on business performance, since executives generally seem to be convinced of this, but on assisting their senior colleagues with what one executive described as the 'hows' of human resource management.

On the basis of our evidence, the HR profession needs to think carefully about its ability to influence and support the wider organisation. There was a generally downbeat perception of the HR function from the HR directors we interviewed, echoing that of the other people we spoke to. HR directors need to work harder at making sure that their function is staffed with people who understand the business they work in, who use language their line colleagues can understand, and who devise initiatives that can make a tangible contribution to the performance of their organisation rather than adding further bureaucracy.

Implications for the uptake of progressive HR practices in UK organisations

Pfeffer, a distinguished US commentator, wrote in 1998:

Something very strange is occurring in organisational management. Over the past decade or so, numerous rigorous studies conducted both within specific industries and in samples of

> '…"good" people management…was seen to be as much about the way front-line supervisors, team leaders and middle managers interact with and engage with their staff as it was about the implementation of particular HR policies and practices.'

organisations that cross industries have demonstrated the enormous economic returns obtained through the implementation of what are variously called high involvement, high performance or high commitment management practices…But even as these research results pile up, trends in actual management practices are, in many instances, moving in a direction directly exactly opposite *to what this growing body of evidence prescribes…Rather than putting their people first, numerous firms have sought solutions to competitive challenges in places that are not very productive – treating their businesses as portfolios of assets to be bought and sold in an effort to find the right competitive niche, downsizing and outsourcing in a futile attempt to shrink or transact their way to profit, and doing a myriad of things that weaken and destroy their organisational culture in efforts to minimise labour costs – even as they repeatedly proclaim that 'people are our most important asset' (Pfeffer 1998: xv–xvi).*

Most of the senior managers we talked to agreed that their employees were their most important asset even if they were hesitant about proclaiming that fact. And certainly we heard many tales of the pressures they faced in search of profitability and efficiency: the difficulties and challenges of managing portfolios of businesses, merging companies, dealing with contracting markets, maintaining service levels despite diminishing funding, reducing deficits and meeting stakeholder expectations. But, even if they were not wholly convinced by the research evidence demonstrating the potential returns from high-performance management practices, most were ready to agree that good people management should have an impact on organisational performance. So why have we not seen a greater take-up of progressive HR practices in UK organisations?

The answer lies in being clear about what constitutes 'good' people management. For many of our interviewees, this was seen to be as much about the way front-line supervisors, team leaders and middle managers interact with and engage with their staff as it was about the implementation of particular HR policies and practices. That perception is neatly encapsulated in the following quote from a 'director for people':

The person who is responsible for people in a company has got four very simple tasks – finding people, keeping them, inspiring them and rewarding them, that is all. And a lot of this is dressed up in huge amounts of jargon, which is fine, but I think it is better the simpler you can get it. And those four tasks are not just the tasks of the people function, they are the tasks of everybody in every company – that is what leadership is about.

We can therefore expect executives' focus of attention to be on the mindset, skills and motivation of line management. Based on the views of the executives we canvassed here, we might expect a gradual uptake of more individualised practices, such as selection and performance management. However, we found a good deal of scepticism about initiatives that are designed to encourage the wider participation and contribution of employees, such as redesigning jobs, involving employees in efforts to improve workplace productivity, or giving employees a financial stake in the organisation.

Executives seem to think about human resource management as a set of piecemeal initiatives, intended to maximise the contribution of each individual for the duration of their stay in the organisation, rather than as a coherent set of mutually supporting practices. On this basis, we

cannot necessarily expect to see a wholesale
implementation of high-performance human
resource management practices in UK
organisations, along the lines that Pfeffer
articulates, unless such initiatives, individually or
collectively, are very clearly perceived to be of value
in improving the way managers manage.
Managing the performance of managers to make
sure that they find, keep, inspire and reward their
people well may be the most critical HR practice to
get right if we are to take a step towards making
high-performance, high-commitment people
management the preferred model for British
workplaces.

12 | General discussion

There are two starting points for the research findings presented in this report. One is the growing body of evidence showing a link between greater use of a set of progressive or high-commitment human resource practices and corporate performance. The UK evidence is based on a series of small, sector-specific studies and one of the aims of the Future of Work study, funded by the ESRC with additional support from the CIPD, has been to determine how far these results can be generalised and supported across industry and over time. That work also attempts to understand how the greater use of a set of practices translates into superior corporate performance by opening up the black box and exploring the way in which these practices have an impact. The second starting point is the findings at both workplace and corporate level, some of it based on earlier findings from the Future of Work study, that despite the growing body of evidence, only a few organisations appear to have put in place the comprehensive set of practices that appear to promise competitive advantage. A series of interviews with senior executives were therefore conducted to try to gain some insight into why this should be so.

The findings from the Future of Work study that are reported here are still interim results. The study continues and there is much further analysis to be done. This is, in fact, the second CIPD Research Report on the project. The first (*Effective People Management*), based on the subjective accounts of managers in the sample, confirmed a link between greater use of HR practices – particularly where they were rated effective – higher commitment and quality among staff and superior productivity and financial results. However, this was based entirely on management accounts and is subject to the biases associated with such accounts. Although management perceptions of these links

are very important – after all they form the basis on which managers take key decisions – they are less rigorous evidence than independent financial data, particularly if it is collected over time so that we can be more confident about cause and effect. This second report presents the early findings based on this independent data, provided by Dun & Bradstreet.

On the basis of this stricter test, the preliminary results suggest that we have to be cautious in making general claims across industry about a relationship between the adoption of a greater number of progressive HR practices and corporate performance. In particular, we found little support for a link between more use of these practices and a measure of sales per employee, which serves as a proxy for productivity. The results using the measure of profit per employee were more positive, but with the sample as a whole just failed the normal test of statistical significance.

Closer analysis reveals that the results are significant in the manufacturing sector; and it is in the manufacturing sector that many of the previous studies have been reported. The analysis shows a link between the adoption of a greater number of practices, higher reported levels of employee quality and commitment and higher profit per employee. It is not sustained once we control for profit in the previous year, so we must be cautious about asserting cause and effect.

When we turn to the service sector, the results are not significant. Much more analysis is required, but it appears that the impact of high-commitment human resource management in the service sector is rather different. A preliminary comparison reveals quite large differences within the service sector with retail in particular showing, if anything, a negative association between greater use of

> **'...the presence of a personnel specialist in a firm has a consistently positive impact on profit per employee above and beyond the adoption of HR practices.'**

progressive HR practices and profit per employee. We will be doing further work to understand more about the service sector.

One of the reasons why the results are not significant in the service sector is that the association between HRM and performance appears to be non-linear. There is consistent evidence across the sectors that moving from having very few HR practices in place to having rather more, reflected in moving from the first to the second quartile in the number of practices adopted across the workforce, has a positive impact on financial performance. It is when more practices are added that any further positive impact begins to disappear. Allied to this, the presence of a personnel specialist in a firm has a consistently positive impact on profit per employee above and beyond the adoption of HR practices. (Just over half the firms had a personnel specialist.) We can speculate on the reasons for this, but it may well be that in the firms in the sample, which reflect a typical cross-section of industry and are often quite small, the presence of a personnel specialist brings some order and basic good practice to personnel processes and this has a positive impact.

There is, then, evidence that basic good personnel practice makes a difference, as does the presence of a personnel specialist. In manufacturing, the research confirms the findings of other studies in suggesting that greater use of progressive practices is associated with higher profit per employee. The policy implications of this are that the more practices in place, the better. However, this does not indicate where firms should start and as we see in the second study, this is a major concern for senior executives. We therefore explored any independent impact of specific practices. In manufacturing, two had an

independent significant effect on financial performance. They were practices designed to ensure job security and an internal labour market, and job design. Indeed job design had a positive impact even after controlling for performance in the previous year, suggesting that it has a powerful causal link. The policy implication is that this should receive priority. It is therefore one of several ironies in the combined studies that senior executives were very doubtful about emphasising job design and somewhat unsure what it meant in practice.

The second part of the research – the interviews with senior, board-level executives – was designed to find out more about how key policy-makers viewed the relationship between human resource management and performance and how far research or other factors shaped their approach to people management. It is worth pointing out that these executives were mostly employed in large organisations of a size that is not typical of British industry. Therefore any attempt to make a direct link between the two studies should bear in mind that we are not comparing like with like.

At least half of the executives were not aware of the research linking human resource management and corporate performance. HR directors were more aware of it than their senior colleagues but apparently did not, in most cases, share it with these colleagues. This is of significance because our questioning revealed that internal contacts were cited most frequently as the source of new ideas. As other research has indicated, most of these senior executives were not great readers of business magazines and books; nor were they very outward looking when it came to seeking new ideas. There was very little mention of consultants or of management gurus as sources of inspiration or change. HR directors would therefore appear to have a potentially important role in communicating new ideas about best people management practice. The opportunity to do this is there; with only one or two exceptions, their input at board level was valued. But this input does not appear to extend to communicating the research that the CIPD and others have been promulgating. One interpretation is that they are not yet fully persuaded by the research.

Despite limited awareness of the research, most of the senior executives we interviewed accepted that the general proposition emerging from the research was highly plausible. All but a handful agreed that good people management was likely to have an impact on business performance. It was, as some might argue, almost a statement of the obvious. In much the same way, most would agree, albeit with a groan, that their people were their most important asset, even if they were not always treated as such.

Closer analysis of the executives' comments reveals some important nuances. When they referred to people management they usually meant the effective management of people rather than effective people management or human resource practices. Taking this a step further, they viewed this primarily as a task for line management rather than the personnel function. Quite a number also agreed that because of line management competences and priorities and because of various features of the organisational culture, this task was often not carried out very effectively. To some extent, there was a bit of a blind spot about how far a set of high-quality HR practices could support the line management task and managers tended to single out specific practices such as selection and performance appraisal as most likely to help rather than the somewhat more uncertain returns from job redesign or employee involvement.

The executives displayed some skill in picking holes in the model linking human resource management and performance. They argued that it gave only part of the picture, they challenged the notion that more is invariably better and they were critical of specific practices. Training was cited quite often as a practice at which quite a lot of money was thrown without what they considered to be a clear purpose or any demonstrated returns. Of course, the model was designed to focus on human resource issues, so it is rather too easy to suggest that it offers a distorted perspective. Perhaps the most important concern they had was that it was research-based rather than derived from local evidence. Most of these very senior executives, with a track record of success throughout their careers, placed much more trust in their own experience, in their values and in what they saw for themselves than in any research findings; and if the research findings did not conform to their experience and values, they were likely to be ignored.

An important practical concern emerging from the interviews was that the research and related models gave some indication of what HR practices needed to be in place but they did not present a model of how to bring about change or where to start. The executives were more comfortable considering specific practices, particularly those such as selection and performance appraisal with which they were familiar and where they thought they could see an impact than with practices offering uncertain returns or with any notion of a bundle of practices. For the research to have an impact, one of the further research needs is clear and, for these executives, convincing evidence about where to start in seeking to introduce more effective people management practices. The evidence in Part 1 – that a focus on job security and internal labour markets and on job design

> '**What was interesting in comments about structure was the feeling that organisations have not yet got it right and do not really know how to get it right.**'

may pay dividends – is unlikely to have much credibility since it appears to clash with their own intuitive beliefs.

A number of constraints on progress in applying progressive people management were identified. Some of these were predictable, such as financial constraints, competing stakeholder concerns and day-to-day pressures. There was also a sometimes unstated assumption that while there was room for improvement in people management practices, this was not a high priority. The practices already in place worked reasonably well; or if they did not, and many instances were cited of specific areas for improvement, these could fairly easily be fixed. Beyond that, the business case for doing more could not be clearly made. The irony in this, of course, is that the research around which our interviews took place, and about which these executives were rather lukewarm, was a distinctive attempt, albeit at a more general level, to present that case.

The results of the interviews make challenging and somewhat uncomfortable reading for the HR function. We should keep this in perspective. The focus was on the function and its activities; any function placed under the executive microscope is likely to come in for criticism. Also, support from HR at board level was generally valued, even if a distinctive strategic input was viewed as no more than an aspiration. There were, however, some real areas of concern. One was the quite widespread criticism of HR professionals for their lack of business acumen and understanding. A second was the fear that people management initiatives too often meant an increase in bureaucracy and interference. A third was the lack of specific innovations and ideas that seemed to be coming from the function itself. A fourth was the comment, made quite forcibly by a number of

senior operational executives, that the HR function should lead by example in practising good people management and palpably failed to do so. More generally, it was somewhat depressing to note that the HR executives led the way in criticism of their function; maybe the interviews invited this, but navel-gazing and self-flagellation seem to be particular delights of those working in personnel management. Of course, an alternative view might be to see them as modest and reflectively self-critical. Certainly, picking up on the Wickham Skinner criticism of personnel managers as 'Big Hat, No Cattle', most were reluctant to wear big hats.

Among many executives there was real uncertainty about how best to structure the HR function. There was some feeling that it could be organised differently, that more could be outsourced, that more could be delegated or given back to the line, that it should become more strategic. What was interesting in comments about structure was the feeling that organisations have not yet got it right and do not really know how to get it right. Again there is a case for more practical examples of different models of the structure of the function and how well these structures work. In considering alternatives, it would be as well to bear in mind the findings from Part 1 of this report, which indicated that the presence of a personnel specialist was strongly associated with better financial performance.

The interviews with executives set out to explore awareness of and reactions to the research linking human resource management and business performance. It revealed limited awareness of this research, a belief that its findings are credible, a preference for local sources of information and local evidence and experience as a basis for action. It also revealed that implementing further HR practices in a coherent way was not an important priority and that in any case, executives were uncertain about how to proceed. Given a choice, many would prefer to focus on line managers and on persuading and enabling them to undertake their people management responsibilities. What they perhaps failed fully to understand is that to do so requires the use of a set of people management practices to help line managers focus their activities. All this does not undermine the value of the research on people management and performance, although, as the evidence in Part 1 indicated, that still has some way to go to present a clear-cut picture. But it does point to the need for a greater emphasis on the implementation of progressive people management and for further work on the structure of the function to ensure that it is in the best position to make an effective contribution. It also highlights the need to communicate the research findings to HR directors as much as to other senior managers and communicate them in such a way that they empower HR directors to spread the message with greater confidence within their own organisations.

References

CULLY M., WOODLAND S., O'REILLY A. and DIX G. (1999)

Britain at Work. London, Routledge.

GUEST D., MICHIE J., SHEEHAN M., CONWAY N. and METOCHI M. (2000)

Effective People Management. London, CIPD.

HOQUE K. (1999)

'New approaches to HRM in the UK hotel industry'. *Human Resource Management Journal*. Vol. 9, No. 2. pp64–76.

MACDUFFIE J. P. (1995)

'Human resource bundles and manufacturing performance: organizational logic and flexible production systems in the world auto industry'. *Industrial Relations and Labor Review*. Vol. 48. pp197–221.

PATTERSON M., WEST M., LAWTHOM R. and NICKELL S. (1997)

The Impact of People Management Practices on Business Performance. London, IPD.

PFEFFER J. (1994)

Competitive Advantage Through People. Boston, Mass., Harvard Business School Press.

PFEFFER J. (1998)

The Human Equation. Boston, Mass., Harvard Business School Press.

RICHARDSON R. and THOMPSON M. (1999)

The Impact of People Management Practices on Business Performance: A literature review. London, IPD.

RUCCI A., KIRN S. and QUINN R. (1998)

'The employee–customer profit chain at Sears'. *Harvard Business Review*. Jan–Feb. pp82–97.